Wildcat Women

WILDCAT WOMEN

Narratives of Women Breaking Ground in Alaska's Oil and Gas Industry

by Carla Williams

Commentary by Julia Feuer-Cotter
Arctic Environmental Historian

Foreword by Dermot Cole
Award-Winning Alaska Reporter, Editor, and Author

University of Alaska Press
Fairbanks, Alaska

Text © 2018 Carla Williams

Published by
University of Alaska Press
P.O. Box 756240
Fairbanks, AK 99775-6240

Cover and interior design by Paula Elmes.

Top cover image: Pipeline construction worker Linda Templeton leans on a shovel. Alaska State Library, Historical Collections, Pipeline Impact Photograph Collection, 1974-1977. ASL-PCA-17. (ASL-P17-8034).

Bottom cover image: Large diameter pipes called flow lines coming from a well pad. Photo by Carla Williams.

Back cover image: Carla Williams by Mary Katzke.

Library of Congress Cataloging in Publication Data

Names: Williams, Carla, 1965- author.
Title: Wildcat women: narratives of women breaking ground in Alaska's oil and gas industry / Carla Williams.
Description: Fairbanks, AK: University of Alaska Press, 2018. | Includes bibliographical references and index. |
Identifiers: LCCN 2017059970 (print) | LCCN 2018014737 (ebook) | ISBN 9781602233553 (e-book) | ISBN 9781602233546 (paperback)
Subjects: LCSH: Women—Employment—Alaska. | Sex discrimination against women—Alaska. | Women's rights—Alaska. | Trans-Alaska Pipeline (Alaska)—History. | BISAC: HISTORY / Americas (North, Central, South, West Indies). | SOCIAL SCIENCE / Women's Studies.
Classification: LCC HD6096.A4 (ebook) | LCC HD6096.A4 W535 2018 (print) | DDC   665.7/440925209798—dc23
LC record available at https://lccn.loc.gov/2017059970

SECOND PRINTING

To my mother, Georgia, my best friend and life coach, who passed away in 2011.

A voracious reader and wordsmith, she kept at least one book and crossword puzzle nearby. Her favorite author, Maeve Binchy, catapulted my mom to Ireland where love, mystery, and adventure provided hours of entertainment. She also enjoyed thick historical novels following generations of families through decades and even centuries. Her love of such historical epics inspired me to write a nonfiction one of my own, a documentary about a new generation of women trailblazers.

My mother encouraged me to pursue my dreams and never second-guess. In a time when women often lacked paying professions, she worked as a legal secretary. While employed in a full-time job, she also prepared meals, paid bills, maintained household chores, organized holiday events and vacations, and served a maternal role for me and my brother, Roger.

Her unconditional love, energy, drive, and attention to detail provided the necessary inspiration to nurture my own confidence and spirit of adventure that led me to Alaska and the creation of *Wildcat Women*.

CONTENTS

PART THREE:
NORTH TO THE FUTURE

FOREWORD

A thirteen-foot-tall bronze monument near the southern end of the Trans-Alaska Pipeline in Valdez includes five sculpted figures representing the nearly seventy thousand people who designed and built the project that revolutionized Alaska in the 1970s.

One of the five is a teamster, described by sculptor Malcolm Alexander as "a woman who wanted to be a pioneer, to build something in possibly the last frontier of the world."

When the pipeline workforce peaked in 1975, approximately 1,900 women were employed on the project. Some held office jobs and worked as cooks and maids, but more than half held what at the time were called "nontraditional jobs" for women.

They worked as teamsters, laborers, ironworkers, surveyors, technicians, operating engineers, and in other capacities, performing an essential role in making the pipeline a reality.

The untold story of this labor-force revolution and the decades that followed is at the heart of this book, which focuses on a transformative period in Alaska history.

After the discovery of the largest oil field in North America at Prudhoe Bay in 1968, a consortium of giant oil companies decided to build a pipeline across Alaska, but it took nearly a decade to bring the work to fruition, requiring the world's largest private construction project.

It occurred at a time in American history when women were entering the workforce in unprecedented numbers and unprecedented ways. The pipeline coincided with the social revolution that swept the country in the 1970s and the campaign for passage of the Equal Rights Amendment, both of which accelerated the pressure for new hiring practices.

Occupations that had been regarded as off-limits to women a few years earlier opened because of government requirements and cultural change. The building of the Trans-Alaska Pipeline was a key element in this national revision of expectations.

In some ways it was a wrenching adjustment, since the male-dominated construction industry was not removed from the era of "no booze, no drugs, and no women" in remote work camps.

In the pages that follow, Carla Williams examines the experiences of the trailblazing women in Alaska who helped redefine "women's work."

They sought opportunities to build careers and expand horizons, breaking down personal and professional barriers in the process for all of those who followed.

Facing skepticism, resistance, or downright hostility on the job site at first, many of the women found that if they excelled in their work, attitudes would slowly change.

Williams writes that, in her life and career in the oil industry, the quality that helped her most was persistence: "I had the personality to start a project and wrap it up in a tight bow, where others lost interest and wanted to move on to the next exciting job."

She brought that same work ethic to this book. Her research includes extensive interviews conducted over a period of eighteen years with fourteen women who encountered challenges, some of them unique to women and others shared by all who found opportunity on the North Slope of Alaska.

She writes that those she worked with and interviewed wanted not just equal pay for equal work, but respect, which they earned. Much progress has been made, but the struggle remains.

"Women who work in the Alaska oil industry today still encounter barriers, particularly in management-level pay," she writes. "Yet progress occurs, which attests to the relentless work of many female oil pioneers."

Dermot Cole
Fairbanks, Alaska
May 2017

Dermot Cole is an award-winning reporter, columnist, and author who has written about Alaska for more than forty years. Cole has been a longtime contributor for the local newspapers *Alaska Dispatch* and the *Fairbanks Daily News-Miner*. His most recent book is *North to the Future: The Alaska Story, 1959–2009*, and he also wrote the popular book *Amazing Pipeline Stories: How Building the Trans-Alaska Pipeline Transformed Life in Alaska*. Cole moved to Alaska in 1974, where he graduated from the University of Alaska Fairbanks. He is married to journalist Debbie Carter, and they have three grown children.

PREFACE

The Trans-Alaska Pipeline spanned eight hundred miles, delivered more than seventeen billion barrels of oil, and employed seventy thousand people over an eight-year period. This is the first book dedicated to women's perspectives of the North Slope experience, examining their contributions to the Alaska oil industry during the 1970s pipeline construction and the later construction and maintenance of the satellite fields. No book, until now, has documented how women working on this Alaska North Slope oil-field project changed the course of labor history and women's roles in the oil-field workplace.

Numerous obstacles faced these trailblazers working in the cold, remote Alaska environment. Women field workers were expected to labor as hard as the men and, in many cases, even harder just to keep their jobs. Only the strong survived; the weak went home.

The women who stayed embraced their positions like new explorers reaching for adventure. Women worked on and around the massive, fourteen-story drill rigs moving across the vast Arctic tundra, drilling wildcat wells on unproven land. Like the new wildcat wells, the first women defined this uncharted territory, discovering new paths. These bold women demanded a true definition of equal rights.

Up until this time, the oil industry consisted mostly of roughnecks and rowdy welders. The newly hired females created a whirlwind as the Equal Rights Amendment (ERA) movement of the time inflamed the United States. Remoteness, harsh climatic conditions, and rudimentary infrastructure did not deter these first trailblazers.

This book recounts the words and voices of women pipeline workers. It contains rich, original research now difficult to obtain due to death or memories stolen by age.

No other book transports the reader into understanding the challenges for women in this work environment or explains the day-to-day reality of working on the North Slope of Alaska. The mystery of Slope living is revealed in its detailed narratives.

The book also provides a historical review of oil in Alaska and the significance of this special time and place during the American women's liberation movement.

Finally, after centuries of earning no income belonging to them or earning a fraction of what the men earned, women in Alaska broke through the barriers as trade workers, supervisors, and managers, receiving the same benefits as men. Not only did they survive, they also thrived, with many flying back and forth to the North Slope for decades.

Some of the trailblazers did not espouse the feminism of the day. Yet, here they worked, at the forefront of change. This book details the reasons why these women reached employment heights at this time, in this particular industry. It provides information on the who, why, and how.

By reading this historical anecdotal account of women breaking ground, readers can appreciate their courageous legacy and become inspired to continue overcoming barriers that still exist in the current century. There is no substitute for historical perspective.

I know, because I am one of those women. Published books and articles about working on the North Slope do not offer much about the female perspective. This book includes in-their-own-words interviews from the women who lived, worked, and laughed on the pipeline. And how it felt to live these lives. Preserving the history of these amazing, inspirational women emerged as my personal priority.

I obtained these anecdotes starting in 1997, when I interviewed Irene Bartee, and finished in 2015, with Samantha George—a span of eighteen years.

Interviews began with a simple request: "Talk about your most memorable experience working on the North Slope and your experience working as a woman." From just this one request, the trailblazers began to talk, telling me their unique stories.

A few women were coworkers, and some were strangers. By the end of the interview, we were bonded by our shared experience.

I hope this book will help spouses, significant others, researchers, students, and curious individuals understand the challenges and lives of female Slope workers and how their contributions paved the future for women in the American workplace.

In a current world where some females are still forbidden to read a book, attend school, drive a vehicle, and earn a wage, it is women like these pioneers on the North Slope who provide us continued inspiration to keep moving forward.

ACKNOWLEDGMENTS

I am deeply grateful to environmental historian and geographer Julia Feuer-Cotter, who encouraged me for years to keep the fire lit under this book. We shared the lows and highs together of this project and of the work on the North Slope, cinching up our bootstraps when required and never giving up. Julia always provided an intelligent offering of advice. Without her encouragement, the interviews would have sat in my closet.

A special word of thanks goes to Dana Martinez Parker, friend and colleague, who provided details on nomenclature and operational descriptions.

Thank you to my editor, Catherine J. Rourke, who worked tirelessly to prepare this manuscript for publishing and for her willingness to teach me about writing and the editing process. Also, a deeply appreciative thank you to Dermot Cole, reporter, editor, and author, who read my first draft and remained committed to this book.

Thanks to Greta Artman, Leland Bowden, Kate Cotten, Nathan Duvall, Samantha George, Marlene McCarty, Dana Martinez Parker, Lianne Rockstad, and Debora Strutz for digging into old boxes to provide interesting photos.

A heartfelt thanks to film producer, director, and photographer Mary Katzke, who helped me numerous times with photos and professional support.

I would also like to acknowledge the brave women trail-blazers for cooperating with my personal questions and their willingness to share private experiences. They are the ones who made this book possible. My goal was to write a book for the public, but also for these women and their families now and in the future, one that would make them proud.

Also, to my many colleagues, who share a special place in my heart and for giving me expert advice and training throughout my career. A few of these friends helped me early on and provided the base confidence I needed to succeed. These include Andrew Allen, Kara Anderson, Steve Autry, the late Keith Brashear, Steve Carn, Brad Chouinard, Brian Chouinard, Duane Cook, Brad Cunningham, Rick Germaine, Kate Feir, Jodie Hosack, Virginia Marquez, Blayde North, Sasha Prewitt, Karl Schaeffer, the late Rusty Smith, Duane Toavs, Sterling Vance, Frank Weiss, and the many others who helped me throughout my career. Your camaraderie meant the world to me.

Thanks to my older brother, Roger, who toughened me up for a career of working in a predominately male work-force. He rarely let me win at chess, and he bought up all the red Monopoly hotels, while I was busy collecting green houses, but he included me in tree climbing, field baseball, mine-pit swimming, and barn hay-jumping. It was either keep up with him and his buddies or fall behind by myself. With his help, I kept up.

To my son, Shane, who has wondered for years if I was really writing a book or just pretending to play on the computer.

Last, I would like to thank my wonderful, patient, and caring husband, Don, who gave me years of support and encouragement. I could always count on him to say something funny and make me laugh.

INTRODUCTION

During the time of the Trans-Alaska Pipeline construction from 1975 to 1977, the proposed Equal Rights Amendment changed the social and political landscape in the Lower 48 by suggesting equal rights for women. However, the road was rough then and, in many cases, continues. Gender biases lingered in everyday situations, as they still do today.

The Equal Pay Act of 1963, the Education Amendments of 1972, and the Lilly Ledbetter Fair Pay Act of 2009 have helped legislate equal pay, but most company policies prohibit pay discussion, so discrimination is difficult to prove.

However, in Alaska, during the construction of the Trans-Alaska Pipeline, Executive Order 11246 required federal contractors and subcontractors with fifty-one or more employees and contracts of $50,000 or more to provide the government with affirmative action plan goals and monitoring. Women were encouraged to break gender barriers and work in male-dominated fields and, with union agreements, receive equal pay.

Affirmative Action Embedded into Contracts

Executive Order 11246, signed by President Lyndon Johnson in 1965, helped women gain the respect needed to change the construction landscape to a more female-friendly working environment. The order required federal contractors to implement affirmative action to ensure equal opportunity in addition to nondiscriminatory hiring, increasing the number of ethnic minorities and women in the workplace.

For centuries, race, color, religion, sex, sexual orientation, gender identity, and national origin defined job qualifications. Employers discriminately hired whom they wanted with impunity. Breaking into trades typically reserved for men occurred within family businesses and during war times as well as the Industrial Revolution, but without these catalysts, women experienced little success.

Certainly, accounts of courageous women tending farms and raising children alone during times of war, famine, epidemics, drought, and a spouse's death are well documented throughout history. However, necessity, not free choice, fueled these incidences, which sometimes included mental, sexual, and/or physical exploitation. By the 1970s, women demanded equal opportunities without exploitation or abuse—they demanded equality. In most cases, on this project, they achieved it.

But, even with opportunities, why would anyone head to Alaska to work in subzero temperatures with challenging living conditions? Was there something beyond unusually high wages calling men and women to forsake comfort, familiar surroundings, and conveniences just for a job?

With regard to women, this book answers that question in three parts.

Part One presents some historical background, starting with the discovery of oil in Alaska and ending with the current oil-and-gas economy. After outlining some women's historical perspectives, this section highlights the author's experiences working in oil and gas on the North Slope.

Part Two contains the interviews and reflections chronicling, in their own words, the lives of fourteen women who worked on the North Slope in the early days to more recent times.

The interviews begin with Irene Bartee, who provides the earliest history, and ends with Samantha George, the youngest and most recent person interviewed. These anecdotal slices of life offer snapshots of scattered incidents of living and working on the Slope.

The original text is transcribed from audiotapes without structured narration or storytelling. The order of language within an interview is sometimes edited to join similar subject matter, due to a natural human tendency to remember details out of sequence. Quotation marks appear only at the beginning and end of each interview to avoid cluttering the passages with punctuation. Contractions and clichés were retained to preserve the flavor and authenticity of the women's stories.

Liquor, drugs, gambling, and prostitution dominate the earlier nonfiction publications about the Trans-Alaska Pipeline, so this book does not focus on those subjects. However, because they are relevant to the times, some of the women recall what they experienced. The retention is not meant to degrade a person, action, or job, but to chronicle the period and how these activities were perceived at the time by this subset of workers.

Genuine personalities appear through the language. Only redundant words or repetitive colloquialisms are deleted, along with overlapping narration within and between the interviews. The most interesting narration on a subject is retained, along with the original language, reflecting both the tone and nomenclature of the time.

The terms "girl" and "lady" remain intact, not only because the interviews are verbatim, but to demonstrate how the language reflected the prevailing mindset of this era. Many terms are now considered offensive, such as the references to "girls" for adult women and the use of "Indian" for Native American. When the word "Native" appears, it refers to Alaska Natives. These and other terms are defined in the glossary.

Part Three concludes with reflections from the author and an Afterword explaining the role of these women in society at the time and in the future. Julia Feuer-Cotter, an Arctic environmental historian and geographer, wraps up this section with "Femininity on Alaska's North Slope," a scholarly review of the era and women's roles on the Slope.

Feuer-Cotter has spent considerable time studying gendered environmental interactions in Alaska, researching current and former female pipeline workers' understanding of the environment through archival projects and workshops. Her essay grounds the collected interviews in the mindset of the 1960s women's movement and provides the reader with an understanding of the Alaska landscape and women in male-dominated workplaces during the pipeline construction era.

In her considerations about those women on the pipeline, Feuer-Cotter elaborates on how the social construct of Alaska during this time as a new frontier and for women as modern-day pioneers enabled the pushing of boundaries to establish a breakthrough in new work environments.

Feuer-Cotter provides a scholar's insight on the importance of these interviews to women's history and to future generations of women working and living in remote areas.

This publication serves as the largest compilation of original research on women who worked on the North Slope during and beyond the Trans-Alaska Pipeline construction. By offering an unprecedented perspective on a unique era and an early example of gender equality in America, it serves as a relevant testament to labor history, women's history, and feminist literature.

Step aboard your personal flight to one of the coldest places on earth as we go north to Alaska and the exciting oil boom era.

PART ONE

OIL RUSH

Above the Lower 48 and Below Zero

We are not makers of history;
we are made by history.

—Martin Luther King Jr.

PIPE DREAM: A HISTORY OF THE ALASKA PIPELINE

The lure of black gold for modern humans exceeds ancient quests for cities of yellow gold.

The Alaska oil opportunity began with indigenous people using naturally occurring oil shale and tar mat as fuel during the long Arctic winters. Early explorers in the eighteenth century visiting the North Slope of Alaska made note of the oil found in this far-off place.

In 1901, Alaska's first commercially productive oil well was discovered in Katalla near Valdez by the Alaska Development Company, and production began one year later.

A decade after the Katalla wells started production, World War I increased the demand for oil for war machinery, and interest returned to the prospect of discovering oil in the Far North.[1] The US government declared large pieces of land as reserves, saving oil for future domestic and military use, with private land leasing and drilling prohibited.

In 1923, President Warren G. Harding designated more than twenty million acres south of Utqiagvik (Barrow) as Naval Petroleum Reserve No. 4. Geological surveys soon assessed the reserve's resources and discovered three oil fields and six gas fields. However, the financial viability of these fields diminished due to climate and access difficulties.[2] Alaska's cold temperatures, road access, and barge access were all significant barriers.

Even during the post–World War II boom, with the automobile industry in mass production, the US government and the public remained cautious regarding Alaska's resource potential. Over the course of fifty years, investors profited from a meager 154,000 barrels from the Katalla oil fields. To put this in perspective, this is only one-tenth the capacity of the Exxon Valdez tanker, which transported oil from the pipeline terminal in Valdez until it hit Bligh Reef in 1989.[3]

Disgruntled Customers Sit for Hours in Gas Lines

The 1960s and 1970s brought a revived interest in oil. With the US commitment to Israel's protection during the 1967 invasion by Egypt and Syria, OPEC's (Organization of the Petroleum Exporting Countries) Arab member states imposed an oil embargo on the United States.[4] This embargo initially had little direct economic impact on the American market, but it rattled the American government sufficiently for leaders to begin searching for more secure oil sources, starting with oil reserves on American soil.[5]

More concern arose with the American oil crisis in the 1970s, when rationing held motorists hostage in long lines at gas stations and when the public's appetite for reliable oil for military and domestic purposes increased. Suddenly, attention returned to Naval Petroleum Reserve No. 4 (later called the National Petroleum Reserve) in northern Alaska. The environmental and logistical challenges in extracting the oil there or anywhere on the North Slope greatly accelerated the quest for new technological and engineering innovations.[6]

The remote location, combined with new technologies—and the labor needed to design them—skyrocketed costs. But, with this black gold, the oil companies opened their treasure chests to spend whatever it took to get the oil.

Dramatic Night Followed by Constant Day

Alaska's fragile summer environment requires oil rig movement and drilling in winter, when the earth freezes solid. Light footprints or heavy vehicle tracks both destroy the tundra, which is the dominant soil throughout the oil fields. Small annual precipitation and strong winds are characteristics of a desert, along with extreme temperatures. Biological soil crusts found in deserts across the world and Arctic tundra are both fragile and take years or sometimes decades to recover from a disturbance. Like rover tracks on Mars, the imprints remain.

On the North Slope, the sun drops below the horizon around November 24, and sixty-five days or so later presents a teaser tip of yellow. During this annual polar night event, temperatures drop to minus sixty degrees Fahrenheit and much colder with wind chills.

The vast eighty-eight thousand square miles of land from the Brooks Range to the Arctic Ocean stand quiet and serene, the opposite of a jungle, which is alive with noise and growing; but this frozen icebox harbors extreme risk for the unprepared. The cold is unforgiving and can turn deadly in minutes. Wind chills at extreme temperatures can quickly freeze body parts if exposed. The body will keep its core warm, while sacrificing extremities, like hands, ears, nose, and feet.

Equally dramatic, the summer months from April to mid-August provide boundless light twenty-four hours a day. People and animals come alive with the sunny temperatures, which reach seventy degrees Fahrenheit or higher.

During hot summers or under a manufactured heat source, such as an oil pipeline, the permafrost layers can create havoc. Permafrost is permanently frozen soil varying in depth and location. Buildings on melting permafrost twist and turn with the softening soil and eventually break apart with the forces placed upon them by the twisting. The weight of a structure on vertically melting earth can drop a building section several feet. To avoid this situation, buildings in the Arctic sit on pilings, and pipelines built close to permafrost include radiators, dispelling heat to keep the ground frozen.

Few obstacles impede the row upon row of pipelines, crossing over braided streams and tundra shrubs and grasses. The land's flat, treeless surface extends for miles, interrupted only by earth-covered ice mounds called pingos. Under certain light, mirages reflect fake, boxy skyscrapers along the distant horizon. Shallow ponds and lakes give a false impression of abundance, but only five inches of precipitation fall per year in this desert environment.

Fight for Land Rights

Oil companies wanted a pipeline, but land claims tied up their land prospects. Since statehood in 1959, Alaska Natives protested the state of Alaska's claim to lands and the debate heated with this oil-field project. Some resolution came in 1970, when the US Supreme Court supported the Alaska Native claims.

However, before this resolution, oil companies designed the Valdez marine terminal and a road to Prudhoe Bay, and prior to a permanent land claim settlement for all Alaska Natives, construction began in 1971. This action provided enormous pressure toward a settlement.

The Alaska Native Claims Settlement Act of 1971 (ANCSA) provided relief to all. With the stroke of President Nixon's pen, forty-four million acres transferred to Alaska Native peoples for their own unspecified use. The act provided for the establishment of twelve Alaska Native shareholder corporations. The corporations would later divest into many business opportunities, including oil-field service companies, and become owners of oil production facilities.

Three years prior to ANCSA, on March 13, 1968, the Atlantic Richfield Company (ARCO) and Humble Oil and Refining Company (now Exxon) announced the Prudhoe Bay discovery well. In the same year, ARCO, Humble Oil, and British Petroleum (BP) formed the Trans-Alaska Pipeline Project (TAPP) to design and construct a pipeline to move Prudhoe Bay crude oil to market.

In February 1969, the name of this joint venture changed to the Trans-Alaska Pipeline System (TAPS). The State of Alaska and Standard Oil Company (SOHIO) began the Prudhoe Bay field development in 1969, following congressional approval of a pipeline right-of-way.

Construction Begins on the Largest Private Pipeline in North America

Actual construction of the pipeline—the nation's largest, crossing three mountain ranges and hundreds of rivers and streams—began with laying the first pipe at Tonsina Creek on March 27, 1975. Frank Moolin Jr., construction manager for the pipeline, enforced hard-driving work standards throughout construction.

Bechtel Corporation and Fluor Corporation were management contractors, but neither company did the work. They subcontracted the work to River Construction Corporation, Perini Arctic Associates, H.C. Price,

Associated-Green, Arctic Constructors, Morrison-Knudsen, Kiewit, Chicago Bridge & Iron Company, and General Electric. Other construction companies, such as Houston Contracting Company, built the interconnecting, cross-country pipelines over the tundra, connecting the gathering centers to the Trans-Alaska Pipeline. The Trans-Alaska Pipeline today remains managed by Alyeska Pipeline Service Company, a consortium of oil companies.

One of the more important aspects of the TAPS construction included the James B. Dalton Highway (first called the "haul road"). This highway provided supplies that were the lifeblood for the Alaska oil fields and remains the main access to the oil fields today. Although some materials are transported by barge via the Arctic Ocean, many materials are trucked up the Dalton Highway.

The Dalton Highway allowed the construction of camps along the road. Eleven pump stations were constructed (twelve were planned), with only a few in use today. Thirty camps along the pipeline housed workers who built the line. Many of the camps were dismantled and sold after construction of the pipeline ended. The largest camps included the camp at Isabel Pass, with 1,652 beds, and one at Valdez, where the Terminal Camp contained 3,480 beds. In all, more than seventy thousand people worked on the TAPS construction.[7] Some reports indicate that women numbered less than ten percent of these workers.

Finally . . . a Pipeline

The first oil flowed on June 20, 1977, starting at Pump Station 1 and ending 798 miles away at the marine terminal in Valdez, where large tankers transported the oil to refineries. Eleven pump stations built along the line boosted the oil through the pipeline, but only a few remain functioning today, moving an average of 500,000 barrels of oil each day compared to 2.1 million barrels a day in the 1980s.

The oil development impact to the state was historic, changing the politics and people forever. Vast lands changed ownership and were redefined.

Travel by commercial jet between Anchorage and Prudhoe Bay took more than an hour over the area's 200,000 acres of numerous mountain ranges, lakes, rivers, and villages, with hundreds of pipelines snaking their way across the tundra, meeting together at gathering stations. There, the oil was separated from the gas and water and sent down pipelines, while excess natural gas was injected back down the wells.

More than seventeen billion barrels of oil flowed down the Trans-Alaska Pipeline to Valdez between 1977 and 2011.[8] New oil companies, new technologies, and new service companies extended the life of the Alaska oil fields through multiple new technologies, including heavy oil extraction. As a result, Alaska's oil overshadows the state's other natural resources and plays a significant role in the economy.

In today's dollars, the pipeline cost thirty-three billion. Much of the money over the years helped create Alaska's infrastructure and the savings account called the Alaska Permanent Fund, which has given Alaskans millions in dividends and will continue to fund the economy long into the future.

In recent years, oil and gas accounted for 84 percent of Alaska's total resource production value, with fishing and mining falling far behind at 11 percent and 5 percent, respectively.[9] However, the state's economy fluctuates with oil prices and oil company revenue goals. Opening closed reserves and wilderness areas will likely dominate politics in the future, since oil is king in this vast region.

FROZEN ASSETS: A WOMEN'S HISTORY OF THE ALASKA PIPELINE

It was the call of the wild to the frozen north, a time un-precedented in the history of working women's rights, set in both a harsh environmental terrain and a challeng-ing oil-field world where only a few women dared to tread.

A spark ignited across the frozen tundra, giving new meaning to women's work and empowering women workers everywhere as the women's movement gathered momentum like a wildfire.

"North to the Future" became the call in 1974. The news traveled to far corners of cities and towns throughout the continental United States. It was the new Alaska gold rush, with men and women arriving by the hundreds to reap their riches in the remote Alaska wilderness.

People from across the country packed their bags for the journey: by air, ferry, or the Alcan (Alaska-Canadian Highway from Dawson Creek, British Columbia, to Delta Junction, Alaska). Women and men alike felt the ex-citement and enormity of the pipeline project. Women

fulfilled their newly found ambitions by flexing mus-
cles in the workforce and pushing gender and economic
barriers through the immense baby boomer generation momentum.

Larger-than-Life Union Bosses

Powerful union bosses promised and delivered huge paychecks like candy to kids. The crowds inside and outside
the Alaska union halls ballooned with people pushing and
shoving to get inside to hear the calls. They arrived early
to stand outside the cramped, weathered, repurposed
buildings where dust caked the windows.

Inside, union representatives gathered behind large
tables or desks in a room packed with people. A distinc-
tive locker room odor wafted between the smell of rubber boots, dirt, and cigarette smoke. The bosses waited
behind closed doors in the back, ready to manage disor-
der if required. Some workers carried worn duffle bags
packed with gear, ready to go. The early, raw dispatch
locations served one purpose: hire as many union workers as possible and send them to the pipeline camps as
quickly as physically possible. The days of luxurious
union halls with shiny tile floors and beautiful surroundings came later. In the beginning, the hiring halls were
rough and crude.

Noisy men quieted as the boss men shouted out the
lucky work numbers, for missing a call meant returning
to the bottom of the list. It was all about the A, B, C, and
D lists and list status. If the calls made it to the C or D list,
the crowd's energy heightened; people on the D list who
just arrived in town might land that coveted job on the
Trans-Alaska Pipeline.

As all this occurred, I was interested in a position
for myself, so I found my five-foot-three-inch,

one-hundred-and-twenty-pound frame politely pushing forward through a wall of tall, burly men as they called the numbers for laborers. My boyfriend was a Teamster surveyor, so I knew the ropes from the many hours spent with him standing at the Teamsters Union Hall. Did I really want to be a laborer?

They called for a powderman.

"YES . . . pick me . . . CALL MY NUMBER!" I thought as I stood on my toes to see over the crowd. "I want to be a powderman . . . whatever that is . . . I want to do THAT!"

I found out later, to my surprise, a powderman inserts dynamite into blasting holes.

I appeared at the union hall twice a day for weeks, but my number never came up, and I finally stopped the pursuit and dream of big money. I would, eventually, go to the North Slope another way, but many women DID get their number called and their exciting adventures are recounted here.

Cradle-to-Grave Financial Security

Formidable unions provided financial security with generous retirement plans, which many workers enjoy today. The Teamsters Local 959 even had its own multistory hospital, providing free health care for the entire family. The hospital doled out first-rate care without cost to members. "Livin' the dream," many said at the time.

However, although women were allowed—and even encouraged—to join the unions, such union jobs remained elusive for them. The union men brought the women in through back doors (see Kate Cotten's interview) and sometimes required a personal connection to proceed through the union hall's hiring process. If a woman was lucky enough to find a job through organized labor, the union would sometimes provide mentors. With most unions traditionally structured as men's organizations, mentors were often male.

Making History

Becoming part of a historical event, while at the same time making more money than they ever imagined, brought both men and women to Alaska. Car and gas commercials in the fifties and sixties permeated most people's homes, so employment in the oil industry was like working for a family friend.

With jobs in oil, they could now afford the luxuries that took their parents a lifetime to achieve. Workers imagined buying new homes, toys, and cars on their "R&R." One of the women, Lianne Rockstad, returned to North Dakota after her first weeks on the North Slope and bought a new truck with her first two paychecks!

Plentiful Opportunities

But, it wasn't just about money; women wanted satisfying job opportunities in which they could flourish.

Irene Bartee mentions in her interview how her company left her to manage everything simply because she possessed the skills necessary to handle leadership responsibilities. She went on to become a powerful force, butting heads with Teamster bosses and threatening them with bombs if they tried to mess with her company.

Irene's interview shows how it took a thick skin to survive, and, perhaps, all these pipeline women had thick skin. Living in remote camps surrounded by wilderness demanded courage, and with close encounters with wolves, bears, or other Alaska wildlife, it didn't hurt to keep a watchful eye on one's surroundings.

All Women Were Minorities

Once these women settled into jobs, some workers, especially men, found the new equality standard difficult to swallow. Suddenly, the person working next to them—a person they relied on for safety, livelihood, and a paycheck—was a woman. Prejudice surfaced from time to time, but the remoteness and scale of the project required a young, energetic staff, which meant the males in their twenties were often as inexperienced as the women in positions such as laborers and teamster drivers.

These unattached young men soon learned they liked having women to talk to, and friendships and romances occurred and sometimes even flourished. The men found it easier to promote women's equality when it served their own interests—and equality aside, it was in everyone's best interest, men's and women's alike, to work together in this remote area.

Breaking into a Male World

Women raised in the fifties and sixties watched their mothers struggle at low-paying jobs. Their mothers' generation rarely had an opportunity to enter higher-salaried, traditional male careers—like construction—but this new generation harbored hopes for better opportunities. Women who worked on the pipeline desperately wanted to make the same money as men. Due to Executive Order 11246, companies clambered to hire minorities and women to fulfill minority-hire goals.

With the advent of the birth control pill and the intrauterine device, women could control fertility and pursue their dreams and decide their future. Their work options meant they could make money and choose to buy items that made them happy and proud, such as makeup, clothes, vehicles, art, travel, and property. They deposited money into investment accounts. Some raised children by themselves, for they could finally opt out of abusive relationships that previous generations of women endured.

It was a liberating time and making adequate money made this liberation happen. Opening the door for higher wages for 50 percent of Alaska's population made everyone happy. The door swung open quickly and it swung wide.

Pipeline workers, mostly young people, all lived in the same remote camps, ate in the same cafeterias, rode in the same vehicles, and worked the same hours. Most women were not pampered in their accommodations—in fact, as the interviews portray, some remote job sites lacked separate restroom facilities.

Some men brought skills they learned from a lifetime of jobs at pipeline camps across the country and overseas, while other men lacked the necessary skills and learned on the job, the same as the women. Men and women worked together and made mistakes together.

For women, the work required strength, both physical and mental, so the men would respect them and managers would keep them employed. It also required strength so the loneliness of being separated from friends, family, and a women's community would not wear them out.

Early Obstacles

The working environment framework (Executive Order 11246) promoted equality—including, in many instances, income equality. Back in my grandmother's day, equality like this didn't occur, yet my maternal grandmother worked as a postmistress and managed a laundry business from her home. In addition, my paternal grandmother helped manage a farm, so I grew up with strong female role models. My mother worked as a legal secretary for most of her career and later managed a strip mall and owned a bookkeeping business. So, hearing the stories from the females coming off the Slope reminded me of the strong women in my family.

The strong-willed, like my grandmothers and mother, dominate this book. Although the youngest, Samantha George, perhaps acquired more educational opportunities than women in the past, she is still only one of a handful of female electricians on the North Slope today. Without Samantha even realizing it, she benefited from the women trade workers before her who paved the way, so she could breeze through without much struggle.

Samantha's 2015 interview draws a picture of a young woman appearing to encounter few obstacles when entering the world of North Slope journeyman electricians. Samantha could not recall a single incident of discrimination. Instead, her road included unbridled opportunities and encouragement by coworkers and schooling. She didn't experience obstacles to achieving her dreams.

The story of early obstacles, however, is the one I would like to tell because it is important to understand and respect how these early pioneers forged the work environment for Samantha and the women in the oil-field business who followed. The road to women's freedom at home, at school, and at work didn't just occur; it took trailblazers like the women in these interviews.

PERSISTENCE AND PERSEVERANCE

Not in Minnesota Anymore

As I walked off the plane onto the Prudhoe Bay tarmac in 1981, I felt simultaneous fear and excitement. Where was I? Minnesota, my birthplace, could get cold, but this was a different cold . . . dry and forbidding.

The terminal—just a large luggage room—smelled like dirt, sweat, old clothes, and diesel fuel. Luggage catapulted off the back of a truck and through a cold opening into the room. Like a mob, everyone rushed to retrieve the luggage. The room filled with loud talking, laughter, and big men wearing heavy Arctic gear, which made them appear even larger. They wore huge white or black bunny boots and pounded dirt into dust as their boots scraped across the floor.

I watched how the men grabbed their bags and moved toward the door, so I imitated them and grabbed mine, inching slowly through the mass of men. I was starting to panic with claustrophobia when someone tapped me on the shoulder and said my name and introduced himself as my driver.

All the commotion irritated me, but I acted nonchalant and stuck close to my driver. Men stared as I walked, making me nervous. I felt on display. We walked outside to a pickup truck and the driver tossed my crammed suitcase in the back as if it were a feather. The air smelled of petroleum products, and the ice fog hovered around trucks whose drivers picked up people from the shack that functioned as a terminal.

My driver followed the caravan of trucks, all leaving the airport with their precious cargo: workers. After reaching the camp destination, I jumped out of the truck without tripping and waddled, in my multiple layers of Arctic gear, into what looked like a construction building. This was camp, my home for the duration.

Slime Camp

The driver plopped my bags at the front desk and said goodbye. An uninterested clerk answered my questions with one or two words. Then, someone with the face of an angel walked up and said hello, a friend I had worked with in the past. She told me the location of my room, the bathroom, and where I could find food. I had felt lost, but she had saved me.

The rooms in the camp were either freezing cold or blazing hot. I got one with a light frost under my bed, which later turned out handy for storing soda pop. Bathroom shower curtains on flimsy metal shower stalls didn't cover the opening, leaving a two-inch open gap on each side of the stall, so I showered early. Wooden slats made up the shower floor. Workers named the place "slime camp" for a reason; it was a decrepit site where comfort was not top priority. I will forever feel grateful for my friend and mentor on that first day for explaining everything.

California Girl Goes North

New experiences didn't bother me, but having a friend made it much more pleasant. Just a few years earlier, I had driven a boxy-looking Studebaker to Santa Barbara,

California, from Minnesota. The sunny California lifestyle called me. I imagined spending my days walking the beach, not climbing oil storage tanks looking for gauges. But in the seventies, jobs were scarce in California, and I followed my boyfriend to Alaska, just for the summer. A summer's folly turned into forty years.

Climbing the Ladder

In California, I learned bookkeeping, so continued that in Alaska, eventually moving up the ladder to office manager/controller for oil-field service joint ventures in the late 1970s and 1980s, which brought me to the North Slope on short assignments. I obtained a liberal arts degree in the early 1990s in Fairbanks and worked for a short time as a certified elementary school teacher for the Fairbanks School District. I went back into oil as an engineering aide after my husband, Don, and I moved back to Anchorage.

My engineering aide position turned into an engineering position due to the scarcity of engineers in those days. I worked myself into a lead engineering position on drill site projects. Afterward, I spent many years in the quality assurance profession as a writer, auditor, project quality manager, and director. During ten of the forty years I lived in Alaska, I traveled to the Kuparuk field for numerous work assignments lasting days or weeks. Many of the interviewees in this book worked steadily, year after year, on the North Slope. My time there was periodic, throughout forty years. I learned everything I needed to know from books, supervisors, colleagues, and numerous mentors.

Minus Sixty and Counting

All the mentors in the world could not prepare me for the minus-sixty-below weather I experienced in the 1990s as a control systems engineer. The job required me to confirm existing instruments were in place exactly as drawings indicated, so I spent a lot of time around processing facilities and drill sites, climbing around or underneath pipe and equipment.

In those deep-freeze temperatures, I walked the few feet from the well houses to a running truck about every fifteen minutes. The bitter cold penetrated through the layers of my Arctic gear, which included silk underwear, a cotton T-shirt under a wool sweater, down overalls, a down parka with fur ruff, face mask, wool beanie cap, hard hat with down liner, scarf, silver-colored glove liners, large insulated gloves, cotton socks under wool socks, Sorel boots with felt liners, safety glasses, and ear protection headgear.

If I felt my nose or ears start to burn, which meant an early stage of frostbite, I immediately went to a warmer location. In the cold temperatures, skin dehydrates quickly, so drinking fluids is vital. To keep my skin from cracking, I would sometimes apply Bag Balm, a product manufactured to protect cow udders against chafing. I would rub it on at night, with the antiseptic smell lingering for a day or two.

The one attribute that, perhaps, helped me through the discomfort was persistence. I had the personality to start a project and wrap it up in a tight bow, where others lost interest and wanted to move on to the next exciting job. As a bookkeeper, I spent hours balancing to the penny, so engineering and quality jobs were no different. Some people like to start a project with elaborate fireworks, but over time, the fireworks fade, and the final parts of a project are time-consuming and tedious, so they move on. I like finishing, so I enjoyed the end of a project perhaps more than the beginning. I met my current husband, Don, a project engineer, on the North Slope. We complement each other, him as a dynamic project starter and me as the finisher. Throughout my career, I felt I had to work harder than my counterparts and stay later to remain employed. I worked with outstanding engineers, designers, and managers, so they set a very high standard.

Free Health Care Reigned

Persistence and work ethic paid off for me, but receiving free health care in the seventies and eighties also helped. My former husband's Teamster benefits paid for our son's birth. Not even a deductible. I never knew the cost of the C-section and prenatal hospital stay. No bill was ever revealed. As far as dental care, I have three gold fillings from those early cradle-to-grave health-care days when the Teamster dentists asked patients whether we wanted gold or silver fillings.

The Largest Privately Funded Project in the World

Women who worked on the Slope during the pipeline construction and beyond are now part of the aging baby boomer generation, and many retain memories of a very different time and place in the 1970s where young people converged to work on the largest privately funded project in the world at that time.[10]

PART TWO

WILDCAT VOICES

*The test for whether or not you
can hold a job should not be the
arrangement of your chromosomes.*

—Bella Abzug

WE CAN DO IT!

This book compiles interviews conducted over eighteen years with fourteen female North Slope trailblazers. Although the interviews contain many similarities, most redundancies were removed unless they offered a significant aspect of the individual's story.

Women who started working for major oil companies in the eighties may have had a different experience than a woman coming from the union hall in the seventies. Since the early days, much has changed for workers on the North Slope.

In recollections from the past, there are always gaps or differences of opinion, but each of these women relayed her own experience as she remembered. Some passages contain language references to gender, race, and profession in terms considered politically incorrect now but acceptable in that era.

Spoken language often is rough around the edges. Some sentences were rearranged simply to remove any redundancies or repetition and to make the language more readable. In most cases, the words remain verbatim, such as the colorful language in the interviews with Kate Cotten and Irene Bartee.

Each interview begins and ends with the author's observations. The women's stories are then followed by the author's recollections and conclusion, along with an evaluation of the material by an Alaska historian and how it reflects not only the times, but also the historical value of the Trans-Alaska Pipeline Project with respect to women's rights and equality.

The purpose is to preserve this important history. Two women have passed away and nearly all the remaining are retired. This was a unique time in labor history in which women in Alaska paved the way for those to follow. Women in construction today reap the rewards of this small subset of workers in the remote wilderness of Alaska.

Irene Bartee, one of the first construction women on the North Slope, begins this collection with her recollections of those early days.

IRENE BARTEE

Driving down a narrow, snow-filled road, I reached a log house nestled in the trees. The woman who greeted me at the door was slender and petite. Since the barking commotion at my arrival was more than either of us could handle, she let her small dog out as I entered her home. Irene and I had worked on a committee together in the early eighties, but she didn't remember me. Although older at the time of this interview, she was exactly as I remembered: kind, charming, strong, and funny. Her deep voice reflected years of cigarette smoking, a habit that remained intact.

Irene became one of the earliest female construction managers to step onto Alaska's North Slope. She knew how to get things done and nothing stopped her.

For example, in this interview, her conversation with Jesse Carr, who eventually became leader of the Western Conference of Teamsters and one of the most powerful Teamster bosses in America, indicates Irene's incredible persuasiveness. Her entire interview provides an accounting of early pipeline construction processes from a female and historical perspective.

Irene's personality and strength helped pave the road for other women who followed in later years. She was a pilot, a manager, a leader, and a mentor to many women.

—Carla Williams

All Alone in a "One-Girl" Office

"I'd always worked in a man's world. I have never had what you'd call a female job in my whole life. When I was a kid, I worked in the logging woods in North Carolina and then, when I got through college, I immediately went to work for the police department in Texarkana, Texas. Then we moved to Alaska.

It was 1962 when I started working for Rivers Construction Company [*a division of Morrison-Knudsen, which was awarded construction of 149 miles of the pipeline and eventually became Alaska General*]. It was a one-girl office with a typewriter and a phone. They'd just moved from Fairbanks to Anchorage, and the accounting firm hired me.

I came in for an interview that weekend with the Rivers people—Dick, Guy, and Rusty. I was hired for the job and didn't see anybody after that for three months. I was doing the accounting, the ordering, everything. They asked me if I could do a forty-five-man payroll. I felt it was kids' play to do a forty-five-man payroll.

The only problem—within a month, I had 450 men on the payroll and five different jobs going at one time. There was no money in the bank to pay them, so I went to the bank and talked the president of the bank into loaning me one hundred thousand dollars to make payroll. I had no authority to borrow money for the company or anything else.

It was quite a trying job in the beginning. If I could have found someone to quit to, I would have. I was working seven days a week, eighteen hours a day, trying to just keep up with it. I finally decided to hire my own help and did. I hired an office girl and an expediter; then we started working like a company. By the time I saw one of the bosses again, it was all settled down and quiet, so I stayed.

The average pay was about five bucks an hour, which was a lot back in that day. I stayed with the company for just about forever as it was bought and sold several times. I ended up staying through all the joint ventures and interchanges and pretty well stayed second-in-command in the company for all those years. In the beginning, most of our contracts were state or US government.

"Cat" Trains

We didn't do just pipelines. We did Pet 4, for the US Navy Pet 4, the National Petroleum Reserve, which goes from Barrow all the way across to the coast. The US Navy drilled out there for gas wells used for Barrow. Barrow has had natural gas for years and years, before Anchorage. We 'cat-trained' across and built pads on the petroleum reserve. We brought the drill rigs in and they drilled for oil.

We were the ones who originally surveyed the eight-hundred-mile pipeline. We must have surveyed two thousand miles before we got the routing that TAPS was going to use. Everybody thought they were going through Anaktuvuk Pass, but then they decided to do that swing around and go up the other way. It shortened it quite a bit.

Originally, when they were going up on the survey, they'd have a 'cat' [*Caterpillar*] and it would be pulling one of the ATCO units behind it. They would put them on skids, like sled skids, and they would pull it behind them. Even when they got into the bigger cat trains, one cat might be pulling four, five, or six of the ATCO units behind it. Some of the cat trains in Pet 4 [*National Petroleum Reserve, east of the Colville River*] might have had ten cats out there pulling camp. Then they'd have road graders and trucks and all the other things that the cats would have to assist when they got into trouble, like D8 dozers.

We would haul the camps from Canada to Fairbanks on trucks. Just above Fairbanks, there was a loading area where we went on the ground and the cats took over. This was prior to the 'haul road.' The camps were set up to build the haul road.

After the haul road, the camps were used to build the pipeline. We had [*Alaska*] Native guides who knew the area and, besides that, we had it flagged. They weren't survey flags; they were five-foot-by-eight-foot flags on a long pole, usually orange or red, so that they would show up. We used cat trains and airplanes for the survey.

It was like the old-fashioned wagon trains out West. We would pull the trailers up together and one of them was a generating unit. We'd have electricity and heat. We would get that started, and the cook shack and dining area would be with us. There would be two bunkhouses, a kitchen, and a bathroom.

Usually, there would not be over ten people on the survey crew. They did have a mechanic along on all the trains. There were a lot of the old-time operators who lived all over Alaska that knew the winter workforce and how to take care of equipment in the wintertime. They had worked on the Alcan Highway. My boss worked on the Alcan, originally.

Getting to the bush jobs . . . you had to use a military radio system to get information back and forth to the job sites. There wasn't a communication system in Alaska other than the nearest military radio station. I used to bribe the military guys by sending them Sears and [*Montgomery*] Ward catalogs and all different magazines and things; they were lonesome out there. Communication was the worst of everything all the time, until they finally got the satellites up and running.

Alaska Native Expertise

When we started, about two-thirds of the personnel in my team were Natives. They were running the equipment, the cats, and those kinds of things. One of them was flying a plane; he was a bush pilot and half-Native out of

Fairbanks. They moved the camps and took care of the white guys. My boss was out of Ruby and he'd grown up with the Native boys. They knew what they were doing. The surveyors were mostly white, but you had the Natives to take care of them, to see that they didn't die out there. We had to learn to figure when it was whaling season or fishing season; and we'd better have replacements in there at that point in time because they were going home. As long as we went along with their way of life, we had no problems. They lived a subsistence lifestyle.

Buying the Equipment

We took the equipment up for all the other companies going north. We set up the pipeline camps from the northern section down to the Yukon River. We bought the camps in Canada and set them up on the road, an ice road at that point.

I did the purchasing for the camp equipment, the big cats, and scrapers. I went to Canada, looked at them, bought them, and had them shipped up. I'd been in it for about ten or twelve years by the time the pipeline started, so I knew equipment pretty well.

Flying in Camp Supplies

Getting to the camps was a major problem. I flew supplies in sometimes [by] myself. The one thing that I loved about Alaska was flying out to the remote areas. I started taking lessons in Alaska. The company owned some airplanes and I started flying them. I got into trouble a few times, but I got out of it. I've flown a twin engine up when the cat trains were running for the surveying. We would fly up there and kick the groceries out the door to them.

Those white buildings that they were pulling were terrible. The camp buildings were originally white, and it was tough to find them in what seemed like thousands of miles of white. So, we ended up dumping orange paint on top of them. Then the Canadians started painting the whole thing orange. That's how all those old camps became orange . . . it was to find them from the air.

Generator Nightmares

Our biggest fear was when Service City started in the late sixties and early seventies. [*Service City was west of Prudhoe Bay.*] We had a couple of trailers there. We brought more up and built the camp. It stayed there for years. When we started Service City, we had only one generator. I'd have nightmares about that generator going down, but it never did, and we finally ended up with a backup.

We built an airport out there too, where they could bring in the big planes. I think they tore Service City down. It was one of the older camps—it was pretty beat up. The airport is still there. It wasn't even built for an oil company or anything. We just built it for ourselves to use. We were having trouble landing at ARCO and Deadhorse [*ARCO had a landing strip near their Prime camp. Deadhorse airport's current identification code is SCC, short for SOHIO Construction Company*]. One of them belonged to SOHIO [*Standard Oil of OHIO*] and one belonged to ARCO, and we had to get down on our knees and beg to get an airplane in, so we decided to build our own. [*Rivers Construction Company built Service City airport*].We didn't ask for permits; we just built it.

I would stay overnight or a couple of days. Being the first woman up there, they wouldn't even let me off the airplane. Women were not up there, period. As far as I know, I was the first woman they allowed off the airplane and on the ground and that was only because I was bidding the job, which they couldn't believe either. It was 1969 or 1970; somewhere in there.

We hired the first women on the Slope. Most of them went up as office workers or timekeepers and were physically in the office at Service City. Then, when the pipeline started, we sent a lot of women up there. One time I know we had probably ten times more women working for us than all the other contractors put together.

Alaska Dreamin'

It was totally fascinating, just dreaming of what they were going to do. We'd built a lot of the pads up in Prudhoe Bay for the drill rigs and roads. Brown & Root and BP [*British Petroleum*] were pretty upset with the contractors they were using at the time. They called us and wanted us to bid on the job out at Kuparuk River. It was building a bunch of roads and pads and what have you.

I happened to be outside on vacation at the time. When we were coming back through Canada, we were stopped six times by the Canadian police wanting me to get in contact with the home office. We were in the middle of Canada, so the best thing to do was just keep going until I got home.

When I got to Anchorage, my boss was down in Houston, Texas. I flew up to Kuparuk River to look at the job and bid it. When I landed at ARCO, they wouldn't let me off the airplane because no women were up there at that point in time. They brought a helicopter and security guards over. With the helicopter and two security guards, I could go anywhere I wanted on the Slope.

When I first saw the Kuparuk River, I thought there was enough gravel to build ten Anchorages. It looked like it anyway. It was beautiful material. We didn't even have to test it to know it was good material. I bid the job. My boss was pretty shaken up about it. Fifteen million dollars, which was in that day like a fifty-million-dollar job now. We got the job.

Flying in the Middle of Nowhere

Before they got the pipeline built, the worst experience I ever had was when I flew up by myself in a twin-engine Aztec. I heard all kinds of sounds in the engine. That was the only time I ever flew by myself. I guess I was the most scared ever.

When I flew a thousand miles in the middle of no-where, through craggy mountains, there were no cabins or sign of human life, no people. There were a few moose now and then, but even when I arrived at Prudhoe Bay and was looking for Deadhorse, it took a few minutes to even find it.

I didn't know if I was out over the ocean or where I was, until I finally located Deadhorse. The all-white buildings back then were hard to find. It was dark and there was only the moonlight off the mountains.

I looked for anything human. I wondered if I had enough fuel to get back to Fairbanks, if I headed back that way, knowing that I didn't have enough. They finally picked me up on the radio and turned on the runway lights. All cat trains had radios. They had searchlights that they would turn on for me.

Ice Roads

Everything was done in the dead of winter . . . nothing in the summer. We quit construction in the summertime and were not allowed out on the tundra. The equipment wouldn't stand up on the tundra; it would sink and bog down, so we waited for winter and the ice roads. Water was sprayed on the ice to build the roads up so we could start work.

We never lost anyone to the cold. We provided for them and watched after them seriously. They brought their own gear up and we inspected it before we sent them out. And if they didn't have the right gear, we would give them an advance to buy it before they were sent up.

Taking the Children to Camp

During the pipeline construction, we had the big camp in Valdez called Keystone Camp. We owned the camp and housed about six hundred people who were working on the pipeline for Alyeska. I went down there every weekend and came back to Anchorage. I spent Saturday working, getting the billings out for the camp and all the issues with Alyeska. We were doing construction work as well as the camp. I had the boat parked down there, so on Sunday I went fishing. Sunday night we came home. I carried my two youngest children with me at the time.

My youngest twins were born after I started working for Rivers Construction Company. I told them I was going to take a year off; I didn't know that there were going to be two. The lady I hired to take my job . . . the babies were three weeks old when she quit . . . she couldn't take the heat. They 'conned' me into coming back.

They hired me a babysitter, but before they hired the babysitter on a full-time basis, they called me about a problem. I'd have to take the kids and go down there. I had a boy and a girl, and during the pipeline, they were eight or nine years old. I think that they were in every pipeline camp. I'd take them in and the office people would take care of them while I was working.

Earning Respect

When Alyeska first started, I had a few problems with the South 48 people, but that didn't last long. Most of the old-time construction guys up there were gentlemen. I never had troubles with them. I've traveled with them all over the United States and gone back to Washington, D.C., with a bunch of them . . . Boston, Seattle. I was always respected and kind of a leader among them.

Most of the people at ARCO, BP, and Brown & Root were reasonable people. They knew their stuff and had enough sense to listen to the differences from where they were from and Alaska. I had good relations with all those people.

Writing North Slope Contracts for the Contractors Association

I was working on the second or third North Slope [*labor*] contract—I don't remember which one it was—and I was sitting there writing up the contract. I had talked to all the contractors and sent them questionnaires of what they wanted to see in the contract. Dick, my boss at the time, said, 'You are only one of the five major negotiators. How do you know the other four people are going to agree with what you are writing in the contract? You are basically writing the contract.'

I said, 'I don't know, Dick; it's never happened to me before!' If they said no, I wouldn't know what I would say, because it had never happened. It was a good contract and it was what they all wanted, and we got it signed. It was the one where all the work up there was time-and-a-half—none of the double time, triple time, and all that garbage that was going on.

Union versus Non-Union

I had no problems with the unions. I don't know why some people had such problems with them. The 'pipeliners' out of Arkansas—I had no problem with them at all.

The union guys would go out and work for the non-union contractors. Then, when they worked for a union contractor, it was, 'Toe the line, boys, or else.' So, the non-union guys got the benefit of experienced people without paying the tab for it.

I know that was what busted the back of the unions up there. The non-union contractors needed the expertise and, even going south, they weren't getting those experienced workers, but they could get them right here in Alaska. I'd go out on a non-union job and 60 to 70 percent of the people out there would be union workers. They were working hard for them, giving them all their expertise and everything else for half the pay.

Double- and Triple-Time Contracts

I didn't help negotiate the original TAPS contract, not the crazy contract. All that crazy stuff they came out with originally . . . it was unbelievable, as far as I was concerned, with all those things it did. It wasn't the double time, triple time, and all that; it was the work rules.

Work rules were terrible. You couldn't fire a guy no matter what he did. Before, if he couldn't do the job, the contractor would just send him home. That didn't exist in the TAPS contract. I don't know who in their right mind would have signed a contract like that. It had to be some South 48 contractors who didn't know what they were getting into.

People who got triple time were electricians and pipefitters and that type. If they worked over a certain number of hours on a holiday, they got triple time. Up there, they were working seven days a week, most of them ten to twelve hours a day.

Exceptional Joe

The original team was unbelievably exceptional. Alyeska knew who it was putting in charge. The guy was named Joe. He was one of the smartest men I ever knew.

I never saw him in a coat and tie. All the time I knew him, he always wore that red-and-black-checkered shirt, a big heavy wool-like shirt, and funny pants. They weren't blue jeans, but some kind of brown khaki pants. All the people around him were dressed in ties, shirts, and over-coats, and he would come in his normal garb. He worked out of Anchorage and Fairbanks, but he was in Fairbanks a lot. He was big, jovial, and easy to like.

I didn't have an appointment with anybody, but I went to Fairbanks one time to talk to someone on some contract problems that we were having and couldn't get into any office. I was sitting out in the front office just waiting, getting madder and madder. I couldn't throw a fit out there or anything because I was at their mercy. Joe walked in the front door and looked across and saw me and yelled at me all the way across the room. It took less than five minutes to get into the biggest contractor's office there.

An "In" with the "Big Shots"

Eventually, I got to know all of them in Houston, San Francisco, Dallas—anywhere they were located. I finally got to know all the 'big shots.'

One time I was sitting in the office and got a call from Joe. He wanted me to come over and talk to him about how we were surviving Native hire when other people were having major problems with it. I agreed to go over and talk to him and kind of lay it out for him.

I got over there, and we went to the big conference room and there were about sixty coat-and-ties lined up down the table. I was so mad at Joe I could have killed him. He said that he knew if he had told me who was going to be there, I wouldn't have come.

Infamous Jesse

The operators union was the cleanest union in the United States. I was a trustee on their training program for about eight years. They did the training down in Wenatchee, Washington. The others I can say nothing good about. If you knew somebody, you could get a job, or if you had enough money, you could get a job. Pipeline money was mostly paid to the Teamsters.

I dealt one-on-one on a lot of occasions with Jesse Carr [*Teamster leader in Alaska*]. He was one of the strongest men I ever met in my life—strong-willed, strong everything. He looked one way and expected everybody to move that way. In spite of all the things he was, I liked him, but we fought a lot.

We were negotiating with AGC [*Associated General Contractors*] when they had the Coke strike [*in Anchorage*] and were trying to put union workers in the Coke [*Coca-Cola Company*] plant. They were banning all Coke products. Well, I kept Coke in the refrigerator, and when Jesse would get on one of those tirades in the negotiations, I would get up and go get a Coke. They thought we were buying the Coke from a little two-bit grocery store close to AGC, and they put pickets in front of it.

But on the last day of the negotiations, Jesse was on one of his tirades, and I got up and walked toward the refrigerator. Jesse said, 'Irene, you don't need to get a Coke; we're going to settle this thing right now!'

He was a character. We got into several head-on clashes. It was never regarding wages and benefits; it was about things that were going on. We had an equipment company that was non-union. All it did was own equipment and rent it to itself and other companies.

Threats and Counterthreats

We were going to take equipment up the highway and rent it up the ice road. We got threats against the equipment—a lot of them. Jesse was very strong in that day and age. I went over to Jesse's office and it was just the two of us talking. I told him that I was going to send the equipment up the road and wasn't looking for union drivers to take it up, and he told me what was going to happen to the equipment.

I said, 'Jesse, you've got one of the prettiest new buildings in town; it's a beautiful thing.' I said that he had better remember who I am. I came from the wrong side of the tracks back in North Carolina and the mountains.

Our company had been doing a lot of rock work, so we had enough explosives out in that magazine to blow this building sky high. I said I wouldn't be hiring anybody to do it for me. I said to remember that 'I know how to do it myself. If anything happens to my equipment, you'd better watch this building.'

It was only just the two of us, so nobody could put anybody in jail, and he's dead now. The next morning there were six security guards on the building. Our equipment went up the road and didn't have any problems. Everybody else's equipment went up the road, and there were nails on the road and everything else. They had a heck of a bad time. We didn't have one single breakdown on the whole trip.

I admit I was a little mean and he probably believed me. I wasn't an angel back in those days. I had to go head-to-head with the guys, or else.

Phony Workman's Compensation Claims

One of our biggest problems was with our workman's compensation when the pipeline was over. Through Alyeska, they had paid anything and everything and never questioned anything. When they turned the pipeline back over to the contractors, our workman's compensation rate was sky-high. We were so high that we were in the pool in Juneau, trying to get out.

I hired an engineer to work on it. It was his specific job to chase everybody down, and we were doing everything we could. Finally, when it was over, we had our rate down to 52 percent, which was one of the best rates any construction company ever received.

A lot of the workman's compensation claims were huge and phony. One way you could tell was when a job was coming to an end and you had three or four or five more days before the guys were going to be sent home, and the back injuries popped up out of the woodwork like popcorn.

I started having private eyes [*detectives*] chase them down. This one guy was from the Midwest somewhere. When they took the photos of him, he was totally disabled from these back injuries and drawing total disability. He was out there running one of them big tractors with all these cultivators and everything behind it, hooking them and unhooking them, and he was totally disabled. We got him off workman's compensation real fast.

Another guy in Fairbanks was one of the pipefitters. Pictures showed him coming into the doctor's office, taking two people to get him up the stairs and two people to help him back down. Fifteen minutes later he was in a bowling tournament and won! They figured that if anybody watched them, they would see them go to the doctor's office and that kind of thing. They didn't figure anyone would be watching them all the time.

That kind of thing went on regularly. We got our rate down drastically. They told me that I was going to end up going to jail for invasion of privacy, but nobody ever took it on.

Fishing and Hunting in Alaska

Fishing and hunting was my recreation with my husband and oldest son. We'd go up mostly around Eureka and Gunsight Mountain for hunting, and we'd go to Seward and Homer for fishing. We hunted for caribou and moose mostly, some bear. I was always an outdoors type. I don't really enjoy hunting that much, but fishing, I love."

Irene retired after many years working in construction and spent most of her retirement summers fishing on her boat. She enjoyed traveling and, prior to this interview, had just returned from a trip to Australia. Irene passed away November 12, 2013, at eighty-one. She was a trailblazer for women in Alaska and well respected for her intellect and tenacity. Her spirit lives on in the many people she inspired during her Alaska pipeline career.

KATE COTTEN

Her friends call her Katie. Incongruent with her petite frame, tales of hard manual labor filled her interview. Her muscular body made it easy to understand how she kept up with the "boys." Wherever she went, a smile filled her face, and I could tell she got plenty of practice as she laughed her way through our interview.

Katie's Slope story started in February 1971, in Valdez, Alaska, where she was one of the first women hired. She started in an office and ended her Slope career in various jobs previously held only by men, such as a Delta equipment driver, which required driving over Arctic ice roads. She pushed pipe around during the pipe-coating process, which took a great amount of strength. These jobs required hard work and mental stamina. Kate's adventurous attitude provided a role model for women who dove deep into construction action.

—Carla Williams

The Hiring Begins

"I moved to Valdez in 1969 at Christmastime, while I was going to college. A friend of mine from Eagle River was moving there, so I went along. Well, one day I found three jobs, so I quit college. Because I was there, I 'commercial fished' during the summer in Prince William Sound for salmon.

One day as I was trying to get to the boat to go commercial fishing, I lost the keys to my car. I had to hitchhike to get to the boat, so this guy picked me up. He said they were hiring two hundred men, and he frightened me with questions. I made him drop me off at the hospital, which was one mile from the boat, then I ran a mile with all my gear to get to the boat. They had already pulled away, so I jumped from the dock to get on.

We would stay out for six weeks and worked twenty hours a day. We made a chunk of change, about five grand. So, I got back to town and called my sis and said, 'Hey I'm back in town and did okay.' She said, 'This guy has been calling—he said that he gave you a ride.' I said, 'No, no, you didn't tell him about me.'

She said, 'Kate, he's the guy who hires all those people out there and he wants to hire you.' I said, 'He wants to hire me—great!' She said, 'It's a secretary job.' And I said, 'You didn't tell him anything.' And she said, 'I told him you knew what a typewriter looked like!' I said, 'You told him that I knew what a typewriter LOOKED LIKE? Now I'm NEVER going to get the job. Why didn't you just say that you didn't know?' So, I was bummed and went home to my little cabin.

On an aerial photograph of Valdez, there is this square, which is part of the old town (that burned down and was moved north four miles) where the water came in during the earthquake. The pipe for the pipeline was being stacked in this area. The cabin I lived in was on the other side of this photographic line. My cabin was right on the edge. It swayed in the earthquake in 1964, but it didn't fall.

Somebody had rolled up a sleeping bag and stuffed it with something, and nobody would go in the cabin because it looked like someone was dead. It was always filled with snow. A friend and I got brave one time and cleaned it out and moved into it. My friend moved back to Fairbanks to go to school, and so I was living in this cabin.

Sounds like a Secretary

After three or four days' home from fishing, I wake up to rocks being thrown on the tin roof of the cabin. The same guy I'd met earlier is coming across the creek from where the pipe was being stacked and the dogs are barking. Finally, I get up and come down and open the door, and this guy is throwing his last rock. I said to him, 'Is that you making that noise out there?' I look at him and said, 'Oh, it's you. What do you want?' I was concerned and awake by then.

He said, 'I want to interview you for a job.' I said, 'You know, you kind of spooked me when you picked me up that day. I'm a little bit afraid of you—I don't understand you.' He said, 'Well, I'm from Texas.' He is tall, about six foot four, and about thirty-five or forty.

I said, 'Let me put something on.' He said, 'We can do this right here.' I said, 'I have a T-shirt on; let me put some pants on.' I'm hanging my head out the door.

So, I went and got something on and opened the door a little more. I could see he was wet; he had walked across the creek. I said, 'Talk to me.' He said, 'Well, you talk to me. What have you done?' I said, 'Well, I'm out of high school with a couple years of college and went down to Oregon and did this and that and came home and did these other things.' And he said, 'It sounds like a clerk-typist.' I said that I was building canopies and driving motor homes and putting them together. And he said, 'It sounds like a clerk-typist.'

He said, 'What else have you done?' I said that I worked at the Air Force base counting money for the vending machine company. So, he said, 'Office manager.' I said, 'Office manager? Can you hear me? Are we communicating? I'm telling you something and you are talking a different language.' He said, 'Sounds like a secretary.' 'No,' I said. 'I worked in a bakery and sold donuts over the counter.' He finally said, 'You have to come in Monday for an interview.'

I thought it would be him when I came in for the interview, but this other guy interviews me. So, I go in and interview and we talk, and he says, 'Do you type?' I say, 'Ya.' So, I get the job. He says, 'There are two hundred men and you'll be the only woman that'll be working here. We have night and day shifts. There are one hundred on the first shift and one hundred on the night shift, and you'll be doing the payroll.'

I found out later that the man was the director of operations for plants in Valdez, Fairbanks, and Prudhoe Bay, and he wanted me to be his executive assistant. 'Ya, right.' I almost passed out when I figured that out.

I cross-country skied to work and made four dollars an hour. I got to work at six o'clock in the morning and was there until eight at night and sometimes ten o'clock; that's how I made the money. I made almost sixteen hundred dollars a month, seven days a week. They had only a day shift, so we just had one hundred guys.

They hired a second shift with another hundred guys and hired a secretary, and I was put on payroll. It was intense. Two hundred men per week and everything was done by an adding machine. It was exciting, and I fell in love with the job. I was about twenty-one.

My father had known Guy Rivers and his family since 1927. He worked with him, mining in the thirties and forties. Rivers Construction became Alaska General and Alaska General became very big on the Slope.

When I went to work for Guy Rivers, he said, 'Can you set up an office?' I said, 'You bet.' I lied. 'Can you do this?' he said. I said, 'Yes.' So, I ran this construction office in south Anchorage in a big yard of equipment.

Then he said, 'We are setting up this job in Valdez.' It was Irene Bartee [*see interview*] who helped me out. I called her up one day and said that I had taken the job that she had. I said that I realized that she was a pilot and that she could do all these things. I told her who I was, and we bonded on the phone. I called her up at different times. She was the head of Alaska General, kicking it off. I went to see her and thanked her for helping me.

Joining the Union

I told her that I knew there was one woman working on the North Slope and she worked for her company and they were being charged for two beds. It was two hundred bucks a night, and they couldn't put another man in this room. She said it might be a good opportunity, but that I'd have to join the union, the Teamsters. I asked, 'How do I do that?' She said, 'Go down to the union hall and talk to so-and-so.' She gave me this slip.

I went down to the union hall and there were probably a thousand people in this hall and it was standing room only. I freaked out and thought that they were waiting for me, but I couldn't get to them, so I didn't know what to do.

I figured out where the bathrooms were and next to the bathrooms was the pay phone. I picked up this pay phone and said, 'Irene, what is that number down there?' I dialed the number and said, 'My name is Kate Cotten, and I am here to see blah, blah, blah.' And they said, 'Ya, we were kind of expecting you. Where are you?' And I said, 'I'm right outside your back private door.'

He said, 'Okay, I know where you are. I'm going to open the door. Bolt inside and I'll close it behind you and don't you miss a beat.' I said, 'Yes, sir.' I hung up the phone and that door—boom—opened, and then that door—boom—closed, and I'm in there with the leader of the Teamsters Local 959, Jesse Carr.

Someone said, 'We know why you are here and here's your ticket. Now, we are going to open up that door and you are going to bolt out of here.' So, I bolted out the door and about five steps out a guy said, 'Hey, did you get a job? What's your number?' You always knew your number off the top of your head.

Well, I hesitated, and he didn't believe me. The number was when you were out of work and you throw your card up and it's got your number on it. So, I said. 'Hey, I'm just here dropping something off,' and I made up a number, back in October sometime. [*The unions categorized "out-of-work" members into A, B, C, and D lists. Those on the A list were offered jobs before B and C. The A list group were generally out of the work the longest. Those on the D list were from out-of-state*].

So, they followed me for a little bit and I ducked into the women's restroom. He saw me get bolted out of that door. I tried to be cool, but then I got scared. I got out of there and caught the plane to Prudhoe Bay that night.

Roommate Makes an Offer

I get into the Deadhorse airport at eleven o'clock that night and they take me to Deadhorse Lodge. I get to my room and my roommate has dried her clothes on my bed. So, at eleven o'clock at night, I'm taking her clothes off my bed. She wakes right up. I said, 'Hi, I'm your new roommate. It's late. I picked your clothes off the bed; let's talk tomorrow.'

She said, 'No, let's talk now.' I said, 'I have to get up at four-thirty to catch the bus at six o'clock; it's late, let's talk tomorrow.' She said, 'No, let's talk right now.'

I was freaked, number one, coming up there. It was interesting; I was excited. It was early February; it was dark twenty-four hours a day; and I told her I was really tired.

She said that she had given up a lot of things to come up there. She said, 'I gave up driving a cab, selling dope, and getting married for the fifth time.' She said that she planned to start another business up there and thought prostitution was a really good business and asked, 'Why don't you go into business with me?' 'You know,' I said, 'it's just not going to work out.'

So, I'm sitting at the edge of the bed and my room-mate is getting mad at me. This is not good. She's mad because I won't go into business with her. I tell her it's just not how I am.

I said, 'Now look, they had to have given us a bath-room.' She said, 'Yes, it's right across the hall.' It was liter-ally right across the hall. I said, 'Look, if you are wanting back in the room again, you come and knock on the door, and I'll take a shower.' She said that would be cool. I said, 'I have to work here and so do you—apparently, in your own way—so I'll take long showers.' She calmed down and we fell asleep. After that first night, I spent many nights sleeping on the bathroom floor.

Looking like Ms. Michelin

So, we take the bus the next day and do a day's work and the news travels like wildfire. If there are five hundred women and a guy comes along, everyone is going to know what that man thinks, breathes, moves, and thinks about breathing and moving.

So, on the second night I'm coming off the bus, coming home to Deadhorse Lodge and coming in that little door and it comes to a T. It was built in the sixties; a bunch of trailers. Left is the cafeteria. Right is to basically all the rooms and wings. So, I'm looking like Ms. Michelin with all the gear. If you really think about it, if you flip up your hood, everyone looks alike.

I am walking in and there is a couch there at the T. There wasn't one the night before, and guys are sitting on the couch. I see them when I come in that little span of the door when you open the door—I see them sitting there. They are waiting for me. I thought, 'Oh, God.' I get scared, so I flip the hood up and limp all the way down to the right and jump in the room.

It took me about two months before I went to dinner. I would not go to breakfast or dinner; I would eat a bunch at lunch.

There were these guys about six foot four or six foot five—big guys—they would sit next to me at Surfcoat during lunch where I worked. One guy said, 'God, you eat more food than I do!' I lived at Deadhorse, but ten miles away was Surfcoat, where we extracted the internal pipe coating that was put on at Valdez.

They started coating all the pipe in Valdez after it was delivered from Japan to Valdez, because it was an ice-free port, then they brought the pipe up the haul road to Prudhoe Bay. They set up three plants for this coating process—one in Valdez, one in Fairbanks, and one in Prudhoe Bay.

They invented a machine to go through the pipe to check the welds, and the wheels got gummed up on the internal coating. They set up another machine that extracted the internal coating. So, now I was working at a plant extracting the coating that was put in four years before.

In a Magazine and a Movie

I was working the outbound rack at Surfcoat when *TIME* magazine came up and that is why I made *TIME* magazine. Also, a whole group, about ten people, came up to film us. I didn't know they were coming. When I jumped up, my one hundred pounds became one hundred and eighty pounds from the thrust. That is how I got to push the pipe around.

When the film crew came along, they started filming me do my job. There were lots of lights. They made us quit work one day to see the movie and, in one scene, my face filled the whole screen. My mom was excited. It was fun and unusual.

There were twenty pieces of pipe lined up sixty feet in the building with doors seventy feet. It was cold—fifty below inside—but the wind wasn't blowing, so we felt warm and we wore our Michelin Man outfit. Pipe was four feet up in the air. Sixty feet down the pipe stood another worker.

We had a board—we called it a board, but really it was a ten-by-ten Lincoln log—pretty good sized, twelve foot long. When the pipe was kicked to the outbound rack, my job was to go out there and pick up that ten-by-ten log, drop it four feet, and go back and throw my four-foot cheater bar, which was made of steel, eight feet in the air.

It was four feet up and I had to get it up high. So, I'd say, 'Okay, I've got it!' and I'd yell down the pipe to the other worker, 'One, two, three!' And I'd jump up in the air and pull down, then throw it aside, and we would roll 17,000 pounds of pipe into position.

Then I'd run back and pull the twelve-foot, ten-by-ten timber back into position. Then we would wash the pipe and get a number from it. We used kerosene or something like that and we would take the number down and then it went to hydrocleaning before the stacking.

Sometimes you'd back up and then you'd turn and hear this weird noise. You'd turn your neck and this huge log would be turning into toothpicks and it would come right at you and you'd duck, because there is only four feet to duck into. The sound is so intense when the pipes hit each other. And you wait until it moves, and it moves your whole body, and you are scared to death.

One time I dove off the platform where we stood because I was scared and knocked a person down and took him under with me. He was sort of funny for a little bit, but then he finally got it together and came over and said, 'You saved my life. I didn't understand what you meant; you tried to tell me. You told me what to do and I made fun of you. I was just screwing around. I was almost dead, and you saved my life. I want to thank you.'

The Only "Girl" at Dinner

My friend Pete talks me into going to dinner with him. He knows everyone in camp, so now everyone knows that he is taking me to dinner. So, here are 450 men having dinner and you look around and nobody is talking. Most of the guys have on the most wrinkled shirt that you have ever seen in your life. It is the perfectly clean shirt in the plastic bag that's been at the bottom of their closet and now they are wearing it because this is a special occasion.

They also have water running down their sideburns. They had wet their hair, combed it, put their shirt on and came to dinner, and now they are all sitting at attention. There is this one guy staring at me and he puts his fork right into his cheek. He doesn't know what to do. He wants to die. Here is this one girl and he wants to show off.

I felt so bad for him. He was one of the guys with the wrinkled shirt and water running down his sideburns. He looked at the wrong time.

Working on the Cat Train

When I worked on the cat train, we made ice roads and ice airstrips. The piece of equipment I operated was called a Delta and looked like a semi, only it was three times as big and had six wheels, but the wheels were four foot by five foot. They were originally built to do twenty-four-hour day trips to take food and fuel to remote villages in Canada. They would go over the tundra and not damage it.

We had a semitrailer on the back where we had an insulated cab to hold twenty-six hundred gallons of water. We had a generator. You could walk into the cab of these Deltas. There were two seats, except one was a leather queen-size bed, so that one person could sleep for eight hours, while the other drove.

One of the first days on the job, I noticed an escape hatch on the roof. I asked why it was there. They said that sometimes when you are driving along, and you hit a bog, you'll hit a place in the snow that looks okay, but you drop down about eight feet.

I drove alone. I would drive five and one-half hours in one direction. They gave me this little map and said, 'Do you see these little pink flags? That's a lake.' I said 'Oh, okay,' like I knew what I was doing.

There was no road (as I had not built it yet), and I was just going along the tundra. When you got twenty-four hours of light a day, you could figure stuff out, but a lot of the times it was dark. I had this compass; it was my own. They didn't give me a compass. They told me, after so many hours, I was going to see little pink flags—reflective—where the lake was located. I saw the pink flags, so I knew that I was [*going*] in the right direction.

Beetles Coming Out of the Water

There were several feet of ice that we had to drill through to get water. Luckily, this guy showed up in a Delta from another camp. I was pretty happy to see him because I was trying to figure out how to get this auger down. We had to get through the ice to suck up the water to make the ice road.

I bullshitted my way into doing this, and was thinking, 'Ya, I've ice-picked, but now I have an auger—so what?' He said, 'You sure the hell DO need help. Heck, I'd need help!' So, we did this auger and we got water. And these beetles came up and I was screaming because the beetles were coming up out of the water from this lake. They were water beetles, and they were coming up and froze when they hit the air. The water would come up again and sort of surge and the beetles would die in all these different positions.

I thought, 'Oh no, the first life, and now I'm killing it!' We helped each other fill up with water for the ice roads. A guy was there the second time to get the water, but the third time I did it myself.

One Hundred Degrees below Zero Wind Chill

One time I was driving and heard the sound of a motor-cycle. There were no motorcycles out there, but it sounded just like one. All of a sudden, a hunting party passed me on snow machines. They wore the fur turned to the inside, so the outside of the pelt was bare, white leather. They had rifles on their backs.

Later on, when I was using the auger to break through the ice, I was cold. And I was thinking about this hunting party . . . what the hell were they hunting? I started to get a little scared. They were hunting polar bears, and I was just starting to figure this out. I was near the Arctic Ocean, not in the Brooks Range.

I got nervous, so I took off one of my gloves and held it over the exhaust, while I was looking around. Then I put my hand back into my glove and realized, 'Oh shit, I started my glove on fire.' I was jumping up and down trying to get my glove off, while it was gluing itself to my hand and burning it. It was just terrible. I was screaming so loud, had there been a polar bear around, it would have easily found me.

It was one hundred degrees below zero that day [*wind-chill temperature*]. They had had a safety meeting that morning and the guy said, 'It is one hundred below today! Your eyes have moisture in them; please be aware they could freeze!' The safety meeting was less than sixty seconds; it was the only one we ever had.

Wearing Garbage Bags to Keep Warm

Earlier that morning a guy had to break into my room because I was frozen in. I couldn't get out, so I was late to work, and I was freaking out. I went back to my room and got my ski goggles. For some reason, I brought my ski goggles up there, thinking I was going to cross-country ski or who knows what. But that is what I used that day to work at one hundred below.

The next day it was one hundred and ten below [*wind chill*]—it's the coldest that I've ever worked in. I worked in one hundred below for weeks. When you took your glove off, if you saw a white spot, you would get rid of the white spot by putting your hand on it to warm it and keep working. If you walked into camp and you had a white spot [*skin starting to freeze*] on your cheek, they would fire your partner on the spot because your partner was supposed to watch out for you. The partner would be put on a plane—no questions asked. We looked out for each other, particularly with the nose and cheeks.

At first, I wore my dad's boots and had ropes to tie them, so they would stay on. After nine weeks, I was able to come to town and buy the smallest-size bunny boots they sold, which was size five. I still have them—these are the white ones, not the black Korean ones. They used to be five dollars when I was growing up, then they went to five dollars per boot. When I came off the Slope, they were one hundred and fifty dollars a pair. With the white bunny boots, I could wear silk socks at one hundred below zero and my feet would stay warm.

Bunny boots were the best boot ever made; they could save your life. I had silk long johns [*leggings*] because I am allergic to wool, of all things! Then I had the sparkly thermal socks and gloves. I had down pants. I bought some clothes to go up there and then realized that I needed more clothes.

So, on my second stint, I endured eighty below, but at least it wasn't that one hundred and one hundred ten below. I finally bought a very serious down coat. I looked like Ms. Michelin. I learned a trick from these guys I worked with on the first stint up there. The wind would rip right though you—the wind was scary.

We wore black, fifty-gallon garbage bags. We poked a hole for our head and poked a hole for arms and tucked them in our clothes. We had one or two layers under the bags and one or two layers over. They kept the wind from coming through our chest.

I wore a silk T-shirt and another shirt over it, then I did the plastic garbage bag. Then I did a heavy thing, then I did the big coat. You had to be out in some serious nonsense for the big coat. I didn't use the hood like the guys because they had their beards, which caused an awful lot of frostbite when the beards would get cold. You wouldn't believe how dangerous it was.

I used to take walks and would look at the Northern Lights. The moon would turn this blood red. There would be light shows: red, green, blue, yellow, purple, and white Northern Lights. I would photograph the Brooks Range from the airport tower. It is two hundred miles away and the inversion would play tricks on your eyes; it does a mirror-type reflection. I didn't know it would show up in a photograph. I thought my mind was playing tricks on me.

Beer for Favors

One time I was transporting beer in my suitcase on the cat train job and I had to carry it on four plane rides and guys would help me because it was so heavy. They would say, 'What do you have in here?' and I would say, 'Everything I own!' I needed the beer to buy favors. I knew that a lot of them liked beer, so I would have different things sent up to me. Girls needed help once in a while; it was a man's world, and I had this beer to buy favors. If I put the beer under my bed, it would freeze, so I learned to keep it in my sleeping bag during the day."

Katie now lives in Arizona where temperatures are milder; she can no longer tolerate the extreme cold. She works in real estate and enjoys the many contacts she makes. She has a large, extended family in Anchorage and travels to Alaska periodically, but only in the summer.

LIANNE ROCKSTAD

Lianne's laugh came from deep down and burst out, loud and infectious. We sat at her kitchen bar. She offered me a glass of wine, but for herself she poured a beer. I could tell the wine was expensive. She turned the glass while she poured the beer, just like waiters do, and I couldn't help but notice everything she did seemed thoughtful and perfect. Over the course of the interview, she told funny stories and we laughed a lot.

—Carla Williams

Getting the Call

"I went up originally in 1976 and landed in Fairbanks, which had extreme ice fog. I thought to myself, 'Oh, my God, what have I gotten myself into?' I wasn't too concerned because I knew a relative who lived in Fairbanks. My mother had made numerous trips to Alaska before I ever came that first time, because she came to visit family, and I was just never interested. Then, after my student teaching in Winnipeg, Manitoba, in 1975, I decided that maybe I was more suited to construction than teaching.

Through a new friend's association with someone at the Teamsters union, I got dispatched out of the Teamsters. It was kind of a back-door situation. The entire trick was to call a person to work with enough specialty requirements that nobody else would fit. They would announce it to the 'A' list and the A list couldn't do all the list of items.

Then, finally, the person who was designated for it anyway would grab that call, so it was a very dark gray situation. What made it legitimate from the union's perspective was they would tailor it specifically to a person so only that person could get the call, even though it wasn't exactly fair.

Embarrassing First Meeting

In the boarding area, while waiting for my plane to Prudhoe Bay, I saw this woman in a long gray cashmere coat and silk scarf. She was attractive, with raven black hair and high cheekbones, and well composed. Someone, anyone, would give this 'lady' a second glance. 'She must be waiting to board the Pan American direct flight to New York,' I thought.

So, I get busy with my book and the time passes, and I get so engrossed in my novel I am nearly the last to board. As I reach my seat, I recognize the coat in the sea of Carhart jackets. 'Oh my,' I think, 'it's the "lady" in gray. I must tell her she's on the wrong plane!'

I tap her on the shoulder and say, 'Excuse me, but you are on the plane to Prudhoe Bay . . . an oil-field construction site.'

She smiles at me and says, 'I know . . . I'm going back to work. You aren't one of the fourteen new Teamsters called up, are you?'

'Actually, I am,' I said with surprise.

'Well, get plenty of rest on this flight,' she said, 'because I'm probably going to be your boss when you get there!'

Testing My Braun

After eight years of doing all things 'warehouse,' which meant issuing and receiving product, as well as cataloging and identifying thousands of returned construction items without accompanying paperwork, I was chosen as the Teamsters' general foreman of the Kuparuk Main Construction Pad. I was the contractor's choice, but maybe not the Teamsters'. But the Teamsters would live with the decision, along with the forty-five men and nine women I supervised on two shifts. Not all the men were happy to take direction from a woman, however. Fortunately, I knew how to do the job; it wasn't complicated . . . mostly detail. I wasn't a Virgo for nothing!

In the beginning the men tested me. The first time occurred when an all-male, outdoor yard crew coincidentally went missing just as a double-decker vehicle transporter arrived for off-loading. The contract required on-site Teamsters to provide all off-loading. So, I assumed the task without them, thinking I needed to get past this test. I am not lying; I had to talk myself out of caving in.

The crew needed to know that anything I required of them, I also required of myself. I needed their respect, even though I kept swallowing my anxiety. The task was far from playacting with my older brothers' childhood transport truck. However, thanks to a very compassionate truck driver who had only daughters at home, and who coached me carefully and methodically through the off-loading process, I made it through the test. Images of plunging off the top side stayed with me that winter.

Breaking a Sweat

One winter, my work partner and I were on loan to an oil-field service company and were inventorying, cataloging, and demobilizing materials for relocation. A call came in on a day when my colleague was out on BBF [*bootleg bottle flu*]. The caller told me to drop everything immediately and drive the 988 B Caterpillar loader over to another Kuparuk camp. It was URGENT, STAT, GO NOW!

In my excitement, I hung up the phone and had forgotten to ask who was calling or even how to contact them. I thought, 'Where do I begin?' Well, I knew where the loader was parked and where it needed to go, but I had never driven one, so I jumped in the rig, found the manual, and started speed-reading.

The manual said it weighed 95,000 pounds and was thirteen and a half feet to the top of the cab. I kept reading and reading . . . I played with the gears and went two or three gears forward. I found the brake. . . . Okay, I handled the brake on and off. Things were going good. 'OK,' I told myself, 'I think I can handle this.' But, the sheer magnitude of the machine was making me sweat profusely.

I remembered my mother's words of caution on the farm. She said, 'Above all, bring no harm to others.' So, I practiced starting and stopping on the enclosed pad, all the while worrying that the clock was ticking. I checked the fuel gauge and as much as I could remember from working equipment on my family farm. I finally decided I was ready to leave the pad.

The snow was swirling like snow snakes. It was dusk (even though it was high noon), and I was eighteen to twenty miles from my destination. I tried not to concentrate on my extreme nausea. Every fear I had of oversized construction equipment crawled into my brain at that very moment. I maneuvered through the elements as I gingerly made my way along the road.

As I neared the final stretch to the drill pad at Kuparuk, I was stunned to see the entire crew waiting for me to show up with the replacement loader they needed. I couldn't believe it, and I felt a sigh of relief that I actually pulled this delivery off. I gave a silent and grateful prayer of thanks.

I consciously try not to ask for too many acts of assistance from the good Lord, but when something like this occurs, I communicate a thank-you for help rendered. I think I literally 'willed' the load to its destination that day.

Doing Laundry for the Roommate

One assignment I had was at the Happy Valley pipeline camp. The camp had run out of normal lodging and they brought in additional twenty-man camps. These camps had a laundry room and sleeping accommodations for twenty people. So, they assigned me a room but said the only one they had was with a male roommate. [*They said,*] 'But, he's working day shift and you'll be working night shift, so you'll never see him.'

I was there for a month and never saw the guy I shared that room with because our shifts were so opposite. We'd leave each other notes.

He worked days, so he asked me if I'd do his laundry because it was easier to get machines at night. The guys were paying bullcooks [*housekeepers*] to wash their laundry during the day.

So, anyway, I was doing his laundry. What he did for me: the food was a little better on the night shift, so he would leave me the premium food on my side. So, we kind of traded off, and to this day I've never met the guy. I don't remember his name, but he was kind to me and I was kind to him.

Big Money and Midwest Ambition

I was stunned by the pay. My first paycheck, my take-home pay was something like two thousand eight hundred dollars. We were being paid twenty-four hours a day because if a shift ran into the next, you'd be on twenty-four hours a day until you had a break that the increment was large enough to separate.

So, for the first two weeks I ever worked on the pipeline, I thought, 'Gee, this must be how much I'm going to make.' That's how naive I was. All I remember was that I bought a 1976 Chevrolet Silverado pickup back home, totally loaded, for five thousand six hundred dollars or five thousand eight hundred dollars, and I bought it with two paychecks. I thought, 'Whew, this is amazing!'

The most take-home money I ever made in my Alaska career was in the first two weeks. This happened through union overtime rules. You can imagine what my first impressions were. I was just sitting there daydreaming about how X amount of checks would buy a lake cottage and X amount of checks would buy a trip to Norway. It was like falling into a lottery that kind of keeps on coming. All you had to do was be ambitious and willing to do your job.

They didn't keep people who weren't busy; they were the first laid off. If your job was done, you always went and helped somebody else; that's what I remember. That's why I kept my job, because when I was done, I didn't just sit around; I helped whoever else needed help. It didn't matter if they were sweeping the floor. They would say to me, 'I believe that is that Midwest ambition!'

I went in March '76 and left Prudhoe Bay in June of '94. There were so many things that were pluses that made a good ground base for me. I've got the North Slope to thank for a lot of things."

After retiring from the Alaska Teamsters Union, Lianne worked as a purchasing agent in Anchorage on Alaska oil-field projects for many years. She started an art gallery on her family farm in North Dakota and sold limited-edition prints and clocks that opened like puzzle pieces when they chimed. She had a variety of animals on the farm, such as a pot-bellied pig, Bacon, that did tricks on demand, which Lianne used to delight her customers.

There were also two sleigh-pulling horses, two yellow Labrador retrievers, sheep, Buelingo cattle, and a couple cats. After the art gallery, Lianne started a commercial interior design business and remodeled homes for resale. She is currently growing her own fruits and vegetables and divides her time between her North Dakota farm and a beautiful Minnesota lake home.

DEBORA STRUTZ

Debora collects and creates jewelry. She also fishes, photographs Alaskans and Alaska scenery, and writes. She built a home with her mother on the Kenai Peninsula and can handle almost any home repair or building project. This interview occurred in her Anchorage home, where she spent most of her time. When I approached her Anchorage home for the interview, it looked like an oceanfront residence, with shells, glass floats, nets, and other fishing gear surrounding the stairs to the entrance.

Capitalizing on the strengths garnished from her independent nature while working on the Slope, Debora used her intelligence and Iñupiat values to overcome gender stereotypes, along with black and Native prejudices. Like the Alaska Native generations before her, she prioritized safety and the importance of understanding snow and ice. She described in detail what it was like to work as a bus driver with a pipeline crew and how important her role was for the successful completion of the large project.

—Carla Williams

Wearing a Spirit Bag

"I was born and raised in Anchorage, and when I was nineteen I joined the Teamsters Union and was dispatched on several local jobs. In 1975, I was dispatched to work on the TAPS project. I worked on the TAPS from 1975 to 1977. I was twenty-three years old when I started my pipeline experience; I was dispatched to Coldfoot Camp in Section Four. I went back for winter work, which was

January 25 through April 15 and, in Prudhoe Bay, from 1999 through 2001.

After taking many safety classes in Anchorage, I packed up the bare necessities and PPE [*personal protective equipment*] and, before I knew it, I was on a plane to Prudhoe Bay, the Arctic of Alaska. When I arrived, I could be whoever I wanted to be. People didn't know you; they only saw what you presented to them.

You didn't have your family with you; you built a family of pipeline workers. Some people returned home on a regular basis and lived the life they still had there, and then they went home and became a stranger in their own house. After a while, people continued returning to the Slope, going further and further away from their families.

I was dispatched on different jobs but remained in Alaska, which made a big difference. I wore a spirit bag and had my Native heritage and, in Prudhoe Bay, prayed every night with my son over the phone. This was my first experience with the word 'minority.'

Using Code Words to Communicate

If you acted like a lady, they treated you like a lady. I was blessed to have met such women like myself working. It was a small sisterhood, where we met in the field and went on to do our jobs, although knowing we could call on each other at any time if we needed help.

While driving the bus, I spent twelve to fourteen hours a day with my crew. Working with guys, we formed a family, and I was the mom. There were code words to use on the radio as to what was happening on the job. There was a lot of loyalty to your crew, which was essential.

If something happened, if we had an accident of some kind, there were certain words that I used to talk to the foreman on the radio, and he would be right there on the bus where the guys were working. Words like . . . 'I have some paperwork you need to sign right now.' He would not know what the situation was, but he knew it was not something I could handle. Somebody needed medical help, or something happened on the job, because the radio conversation up there was monitored by everyone.

When you were a bus driver, it was a loyalty thing to your crew and foreman. They wanted everything to run perfectly smooth on the job for the people they worked for. So, on the radio you were not a sissy; you didn't cry wolf. You didn't say things that might not be true. It might not be the situation you thought it was, so you called for the foreman, and he would handle the situation.

The secret was to never find yourself in a compromising situation. Women on the Slope were few and far between. You had to be polite, excuse yourself, and go to your room or the recreation room as fast as you could. The more people around, the less aggressive the men were. You didn't want to get yourself stuck in a situation in someone's room alone, so men could make advances toward you. You stuck with the crowds.

My job was to get the crews gathered in the bus, be available for the contractor at all times, leave camp on time, drive, and arrive on the job, usually right after the foreman. [*It is thirty-four miles from Kuparuk Camp to Alpine.*] As the day progressed, the bus driver, being seated in a higher position, would watch the crew for signs of anything of importance, such as an accident or polar bears.

Twelve to Fourteen Hours a Day for Eight Weeks

The winter conditions were all new to me when I started. Like whiteout phases . . . phase one, two, and three. When caught out on the job, sometimes there would be only five-minute warnings. Everyone was to pile onto the bus.

It was as if we had been placed in a room with no walls; nothing could be seen outside the bus. I could see all the eyes in the back of the bus looking forward to me in the rearview mirror, wondering what was going to happen next. We would be escorted back to camp by a 988 loader [*thirty-five-foot-long, thirteen-foot-high dirt/snow moving equipment with large bucket*]. It took several hours, and we would get back too late for dinner.

After cleaning the bus, I would go to my room exhausted, lay on my bed, and fall asleep with my clothes on. I believe hauling the people on the Slope was a very important job. I was responsible for their lives when they were on my bus. My crew felt safe with me. When we left camp, they would fall asleep and sleep until I would slow the bus down and was approaching the job.

Driving on the Firing Line

In the beginning of the TAPS job, we were scheduled to work eight weeks on and two weeks off. This meant you were working twelve to fourteen hours for eight weeks and home for two. When I worked on the Slope January 25 through April 15, my job depended on the ground staying frozen on the tundra. Nowadays, many year-round [*noncraft*] employees work 'two on and two off.'

My son was only ten years old and home with his dad, so when I would talk to him in the evening and, if he needed me to come home, the superintendent knew he needed to get someone else lined up. They would usually call the hall in Anchorage and send somebody up. It didn't take long at all.

Being a bus driver at the firing line, you had to travel; you moved the bus every eight minutes to stay on top of where the guys were. If they needed to get on the bus for something, they wanted you right there. If they stopped the line or found a few minutes where the guy was welding and the guy backing him didn't have to be there, he would run to get on the bus to get some gloves that weren't wet.

If his face mask was all frosted up and he couldn't breathe because it was starting to freeze to his face, he needed to get on the bus, change out some of his gear, and get right back off the bus and back in line. The work was like a big wheel when you worked with these guys. Everyone had his or her position, and you stayed in your position. If you needed to get out of position, you let someone know. Everybody felt like they were taken care of, and they would take care of the other guys.

When I would leave camp with all aboard, I would turn up the heat in the bus and everyone would fall asleep; nobody told me how to drive. Sometimes I would be able to see the sun coming up; it would be like I was there by myself. I would turn the heat down when they went to sleep. Then I would approach the job and slow the bus down and brake, so they would feel it and be woken up and ready when the foreman came onto the bus. When the foreman came onto the bus, we would have daily safety meetings every morning. Some days we drove all the way from Kuparuk to Alpine.

As a bus driver, I dried and sewed mittens and headgear and kept track of the crew and temperatures that reached forty below. It was impossible for them to open the door to the bus due to the heavy Arctic gear they were required to wear, so I would open and close the door every time someone wanted in or out. I wanted to talk to them about their home, kids, school—trying to keep a positive attitude. You asked about things they wanted to hear about; you kept an open ear.

Hugging the foreman in front of the crew when the job was done was always a little embarrassing for me because you kept yourself at a distance from the people for months. So, when you hugged the foreman, the crew all gave a round of applause; it was nice.

When I was sitting in the driver's seat of my bus at Alpine Camp, a gentleman I worked for was standing behind the bus. The bus was at least forty feet long, and he kept tapping his butt. Finally, I said, 'What do you want? I don't know what you are saying!' He said, 'I want you to back up the bus, Debbie.' I had no idea. I was so embarrassed for him trying to give me directions.

Looking for a Letter

Guys wanted to touch me like reaching out for a parent. I was in charge of their mail, food, and coffee. I dried their face masks, sewed things, listened to their problems. I was always there when they needed me.

When they got those letters from home, you could tell what was in the letter by the expression on their face or if they jumped up to get off the bus to be ready for work. She was seeing somebody else. She decided things about the kids, and he wasn't involved in the decision because he wasn't there. The mom wore all the hats when these guys were up North working. She made all the decisions for the family, the home, her own job. These guys weren't part of it.

So, the mail was the first thing in the morning. I would go to the office to get the mail and get it back to the bus. Then as the guys got on, I would pass out the letters to them. Some guys never got letters, and they were always looking for them.

Talking like a Man

One embarrassing moment was when I spent several hours on the bus with some people from the deep South and the conversation turned to things at home. Then they talked disparagingly about African Americans, calling them names. This really stunned me to hear people talk this way. When I was in high school in 1969, we had the first black people in my high school. So, when these guys were talking like this, I was shocked and embarrassed.

Then there is what I refer to as 'fuck talk.' For the most part, the guys kept it to a minimum while I was around. But there was an occasion where I had to speak out. There was this one guy, a young kid. I don't know why, but every morning he had to be on the bus yelling, and every other word was the 'F' word.

So, finally I got tired of it. I turned around and stood up and said, 'Do you think we are all so stupid that we are limited to conversation such as you are giving us? Don't you think we all know how to talk?' He got the message right away. First thing in the morning, we did not need to listen to such rude conversation.

While I was attending a safety meeting on this same job, there were two workers who were harassing the safety representative. I turned around and said, 'Shut up, so we can get this information and get out of here.' Sometimes you needed to speak like one of the guys, not a woman. I didn't want to say, 'Your mother would not want to hear you talking like that!' If the foreman was around, they didn't talk that way.

Safety Depending upon Everyone Else

Everyone depended upon everyone else to be alert, have enough sleep, and not be depressed. Sometimes guys would get depressed.

Everyone needed to pay special attention when moving equipment because if they were lifting a welding shack and moving it to the next section of pipe and setting it down, the workers needed to know everyone's next move.

If they lifted the shack too fast, they would have welding equipment falling off.

Or, if there was somebody in front of the rig who was not supposed to be there, and we noticed the operator was watching the shack and not the person, then we could say something to the operator. The company wanted everyone to go back in the same condition they came out in and they really pushed it.

Communication was almost impossible once we were off the bus and had all our gear on, with the wind blowing and the darkness. If there were changes in the arrangement, they needed to be made ahead of time, so everyone was aware. During the morning, they had a safety meeting where everybody said what they thought and discussed concerns.

When everybody got dressed and got off the bus, the plan could not be changed. So, if the foreman had something else going on, we'd all get back on the bus, and he'd be talking to them all at one time.

Ice Road Cracks as Wide as a Boot

I worked on one job where we went out to Seal Island. The road was made on top of the ocean. They would spray it with water, then it would freeze. Then they would spray it, and it would freeze again. Every morning we would drive on the land out to where the ice road started, which was on the Bering Sea. Seal Island was about seven miles out from land.

There were some mornings, as I approached the ice, I could see the cracks were wide as my bunny boots. It would kind of freak me out because I was responsible for these people on the bus, not only myself. I had a door to escape out if I needed it. The guys behind me did not.

There was never a need, until we got to this job, to even consider using the back door of the bus. I was usually pulling a generator or something else behind the bus, so we never used the back door. The backhoes used on this job would dig out a trench, and they would set the pipeline into the trench, so it sat on the ground under the ocean. The operators on the job had releases made inside the cab where they sat for escaping the rig if it were to go through the ice.

I was very concerned about the ice. I would call the ice doctor [*colloquial term*], who was a specialist from Canada, and he would come and check out the ice to make sure it was safe. I wanted someone else to be responsible for the condition if it were to happen. I was the driver and not qualified.

The ice doctor was usually on-site already for one reason or another. He was a specialist. I never really got to chat with him much. He would be standing outside the bus and say, 'What's up, Debbie?' I'd say, 'There's a big crack here.' He would look at it and assess if it happened during the night and what it looked like farther down. He would make the judgment call whether I would drive the bus out there or not.

Preserving the Peace at Home

When I was a mom at home with Eric for the first ten years of his life, I made up a lot of stories about flying squirrels and beavers.

We lived near the Prince Hotel in Girdwood, so we imagined how Billy and Bobby Beaver would go into the swimming pool late at night, when nobody was there, and they would sneak in and sneak out. We would talk about the owl who had the squirrel on his back and the squirrel had on goggles and they flew over Potter's Marsh into Anchorage. The squirrel pats the owl and says, 'Slow down a little bit; I think I have a call,' and he would pull out his cell phone.

All the stories Eric and I made up had a legend to them. There were thirty-two of them. I talked to Eric every night on the phone, and we would say our prayers. Walking down the hall to work one morning, I asked the guy from the room next to mine, 'Do you hear Eric and I praying?' 'No,' he said, 'but I hope you are praying for all of us.'

'Prudhoe Bay to Homer,' was my answer.

One time my son called, and I went home; it was right around Easter. He and his father were having some difficulties, so I went to the sporting goods store and bought a tent. We put up the tent in the living room, so when they had a conflict, one could go into the tent with the dog, Loulou, and the other one wouldn't see the other one. It was kind of like a safety zone.

Bringing Warmth through the Stickmen

While I was in town, the company was in Alpine with all the other crews. People were putting up electrical lines and buildings. When we first arrived at Alpine, there was only one drill rig, a small camp, and a cafeteria. I would drive to the cafeteria to get some treats for the guys, use the restroom, and get right back.

Now, at the end of this job I am talking about, the place was packed with people. I couldn't even bring the bus in there anymore. There were people climbing over each other to get their portion of the jobs completed.

When I went to town at Easter, I was there for three days. When I came back, I had some Hawaiian clothes, shorts, sunglasses, and baseball caps, and I got with the carpenter and he cut two stick figures. I dressed them in the shirts, sunglasses, and baseball caps, and we had them with their hands up and holding a reflective sign that read 'slow down' or 'stop.'

In that area of Alaska, there are no trees. There are very few bushes, so the stickmen stood out. I'm sure that everyone has a picture of themselves with the stickmen. I won a safety award because of how important the stickmen were to job safety.

Waiting for the Sunrise

When we went up in January, daylight was very short. We used the headlights from the bus for a lot of different things . . . for people to see and locate items. During stab-in and bolting, I drove behind two laborers who were out walking, so we could use the headlights to try and locate the hole covers. They had to clean them off, flip them open, and make sure they were on the hole.

Then, the people who were stab-in and bolting would come right behind us. This was the hole the VSM [*vertical support member*] goes in. First, the surveyors went out and marked the trail. Then came the drill rig and it drilled down for the VSM. They bolted the top section on the crossbeam, then they came along with a side boom, picked up the crossbeam, and placed it in the hole. Then the slurry [*cement*] crew filled around the pipe, so it was permanent.

At the job site in the morning, they had all the rigs, side booms, and cranes started up and—chug, chug, chug—a lot of exhaust. Once you started moving, or the wind picked up, the exhaust moved.

There were so many shades of white up there it was amazing. You'd get out of the bus and there would be a track of another vehicle and everything blended together. A ptarmigan would jump up out of the track and scare you to death, because you don't see them because they are white, too.

The white foxes were hard to see. You never wanted to get too close to those animals because they were always looking for food. Once you got bitten, you'd have to go through the series of stomach shots and probably not stay on the job for very long. The white fox lived under the barracks at Kuparuk.

We waited a long time for the sunrise, so when it came, it was like, 'God didn't forget this place!' It was amazing after you'd been there for a month in the dark. You really realized what the Alaska Native people had to go through having to live in the dark in Alaska. The tundra was endless. You'd see the horizon and maybe there wasn't anything after it; it would just be the end. You looked at things differently up there.

Sometimes when the sun started coming up again, it was amazing because the ice roads were solid ice. You weren't allowed to have studs or chains; you just had to learn how to drive on the ice. Another crew would come and spray it, so it was like a mirror.

You learned the weight of your bus. You learned how to compensate when you started to slide. But you always knew, if you ran into trouble, all you had to do was call the foreman because you needed to get the crew where it was supposed to be. If they were not there on time, the project would lose money and it would look bad for the company.

No Studs, No Chains—Just Guts

When I first started driving up there, it was very hard. I was surprised they didn't use chains or studs. Sometimes they had the delineator [*reflective safety posts*] on the side of the road. The road itself was double wide; then, the road would usually drop off at about four feet. If you were driving, especially at night, coming and going with the crew, you would lose sight of those delineators, or the wind would be blowing, and you couldn't see them.

People who worked in that area for a long time knew the roads. If you were a new driver, you had to drive slower. I did in the beginning, but after a while I learned the bus and knew when I was leaving camp. The foreman left camp right before me, so he knew I was on the road.

There were times when we slid; I won't say there weren't. When they 'hot-mopped' the road (applied water to ice roads to repair cracks), usually there were signs up. But, if the wind had blown the signs down, you'd find yourself driving on a mirror. And right next to that mirror was the pipeline, so you did the best you could. I never got into a bad situation I could not get myself out.

Coveted Conveniences

When I was working with the firing line, which were the welders, the foreman on the jobs treated those specialty people well. So, behind the bus, in tow, was a generator, because we had a coffee maker and a microwave on the bus. The guys would take over two or three seats. The carpenter would build a flat table and on those two and three seats there was a small microwave and large coffee pot. Before the guys got on the bus at break, I would grind the coffee beans. The guys really appreciated the fresh-ground coffee.

I would bring different things on the bus from dinner the night before, such as vegetables, cheese, and crackers. They really appreciated all the effort. Once, when I went to town and got back, the bus driver said, 'Ya know, it was really hard to handle those people you've spoiled so badly.' But, I just kind of figured it was part of the job, and I had the time.

Visiting the Only Store

People from different parts of Kuparuk would sometimes want to go to the store in Deadhorse, so that would be a sixteen-hour day. We would all pile on the bus, and I'd take them to Deadhorse, which was an hour's drive. Sometimes the store would almost be closed, so we'd all rush in. We would call and tell them we were coming because it was the only store people had besides the commissary. They would buy televisions and other things; it was very expensive there.

Losing Windshield Wipers in a Whiteout

We did run into some whiteout situations which really scared me because I had never been in a whiteout before. It came on in about five minutes. They could see it coming from the Alpine area and it would engulf the job site. All the people would leave their pickup trucks and get onto the bus, so we could have a head count.

When you looked out the windows of the bus, you couldn't see anything; it was blowing snow sideways. It was like you were in a little room with all these people. We probably could have survived for a couple days with the supplies we had on the bus. A couple of times the weather was so bad we lost our windshield wipers.

The inside of the bus fogged up because there were so many people. So, you had one guy wiping your windshield, and you were trying to watch taillights in front of you, because if you lost those taillights, you could go off the road, and it may be some time before you were rescued and got back on the road.

As I was driving, they would try to clear the windshield from the inside and outside. They would just open the door and reach across the bus. There was so much moisture inside the bus with the wet bodies and wet clothes, we'd have to drive with the window on the driver's side and the door half open to cause a breeze across.

Then we'd lose the wipers, and I'd call the mechanic and he'd say, 'Debbie, I'd really like to help you, but I lost mine down the road a while ago.' So, trying to focus on the taillights was really hard. When I got back to camp, my eyeballs felt like they were on my cheeks. It took us a couple hours to get back, when it took twenty minutes to get out to the job site. We could only go about five miles an hour.

All the guys were very appreciative when I pulled up into camp. They climbed off the bus, thanking me for the safe ride home. It would just be me sitting there on the bus and I'd think, 'Oh, dear God, thank you for watching over us.' I'd clean the bus, dump the garbage, park the bus, and it is amazing what you can do when you have to do it. The next morning, we'd all pile back on the bus.

Cardboard Cubbies

The buses were four-wheel-drive school buses. There was nothing fancy about them. The guys would have a whole seat to themselves, and there were about thirty seats on the bus. They would put their stuff down on the floor and tuck things under the seat. I would save cardboard and then they would duct-tape it to the window, so it would insulate it. So, cardboard was a 'hot item.' Everybody's little cubby space was their own. It was like a small mobile hotel.

There was one time when I was pulling not only a generator, but also an outhouse with me. That was tricky trying to get turned around. The guys all got a big laugh when I would try to get in a small space. There were a lot of things I had to learn. I took it in stride, because being the new guy on the block and being a woman, it was something I had to do.

Bringing Love Home through a Pillowcase

In the mess hall, there were fifty tables and most of them were filled with guys. A lot of times I would get my food to go. I spent time after work in my room because I didn't want to be hanging around the camp with the guys.

Every once in a while, we would get stuck out on the job, and I would have a cloth bag with me. In the bag, I had a pillowcase with something drawn on it. One pillowcase was the Alpine sign; other ones were of animals and fish and things like that. I would make up stories for Eric relating to the pillowcase, and I would send the stories home to him. He would hide them underneath his mattress and save them until I got back so we could read them together. When I came back, I'd have a new pillowcase for him for his bed.

At that time, we lived in Girdwood, so Eric and I would lay on his bed and watch the Northern Lights at night. He wouldn't let anyone else read them until I got home, and he would pull them out from underneath the bed. We would read the stories together; he looked forward to those stories."

***

Debora commutes from her house in Anchorage to the Kenai Peninsula where she built a second home. Debora's dream is European travel, but in the meantime, she spends her time maintaining her homes, fishing, and creating beautiful art.

NORMA CARTER

I interviewed Norma in her Washington State home, which was meticulously decorated with beautiful and tasteful furnishings. We listened to a big band orchestra on her new Bose stereo and talked at the dining room table. Her hair was a shimmering gray and perfectly coiffed. She smiled nearly the entire time I was there; it was apparent she liked to talk about her experiences.

Norma was older than most personnel when she started working on the Slope. She was interested in the culture as well as the money, and her interview reflects that passion.

—Carla Williams

Bringing Too Many Clothes

"I think it was 1976. I've never regretted it, because for me it was an experience that added a whole lot to my life. I learned so much that was interesting, and by being there early on, I had opportunities to do things that you couldn't do a few years later. I heard about the Slope when I was in the office and they were doing the Slope payrolls.

I'll never forget when I walked into my room. I had no idea what to expect. There was this other girl in there. There was this little tiny room and our beds were so close, with just a table in between, both single beds. There was no place to hang your clothes and I had taken a ton. By the time I got my parka and boots in the closet, it was practically full. I almost broke into tears. I didn't know if I could do it or not, this little tiny room with this girl I didn't even know, being so close together.

It was in Staff Camp at Prudhoe Bay. This girl, who was my roommate, was working for some of the VIP ARCO staff. We didn't have any privacy, which was the thing I wasn't accustomed to. I got used to it after a while and didn't mind it. I liked it better if I was by myself, but you couldn't always have that. Somebody would come into the room in the middle of the night, directly off a plane. We always had a different room every time we came in. The only time I had a room of my own was when we were in the NANA Camp; I had a private bath and shower.

Sending the Big Bucks Home

I was office manager the last few years. I started out as payroll clerk, but for a long time I did the airline flights and billeting [*room scheduling*]. It seemed like every time we got a new contract, I would have an upgraded position, with an increase in salary, which was great. I earned my nest egg up there. There was nothing to spend your money on; you couldn't go out and blow your money on clothes or getting your hair done or anything like that.

I started saving my money and sent it to a savings and loan in Bellevue. This girl, a friend of mine who worked there, would be just flabbergasted I could send so much money all the time. I would just send it down there and she would add it to my account.

I recently finished the last big CD that was paying thirteen and a half percent. Can you imagine that? The bank was probably thrilled when my time finally ran out, because they were only paying about five or six. I ended up with quite a sizable nest egg.

I used to worry about some of the guys' wives at home. Their wives would call our office and want to know if they were okay since they hadn't heard from their husbands for quite a while. I'd talk to the guys and ask them, 'Why don't you call your wife?' Some of them would and some of them wouldn't. They kind of felt like they had a mountain and river between them and home, and they could live separate lives up there and then go home and everything would be fine again.

I spent a lot of holidays up there, like Christmas and Thanksgiving. I remember one time I went to the bathroom and balled my eyes out. That was earlier on in the spring at one of my birthdays—it was probably a memorable one, probably sixty. I just remember I had been up there quite a few years and thought, 'What am I doing up here?' I didn't have my family around me—that was kind of odd.

The Work: Long, Tiring, and Dangerous

It wasn't all that hard to be up there, but when you got to the end of the contract, you'd be so tired. We worked a lot of twelve-hour days, seven days a week. When I was an office manager, I was very busy; time went very fast.

At night I always went to bed early, but I still wanted to iron my clothes, so I'd do it in the morning. I'd get up real early. There were ironing boards back in the laundry room. Hardly anybody used them, but I did and a few other girls. Not very many of us ironed our clothes.

I was a little bit overwhelmed by the amount of work getting done by the workforce outside. I couldn't believe it. I remember that if something came up, like a machine broke down, they'd have to work it out. Normally, in Washington, it would take a week for someone to come up with some idea and put it together and do the construction work to make it possible. The fellows on the Slope did it in about four or five hours.

They would come up with any idea. They were ingenious, and they would instantly scrounge for materials and get the job done and go right on. Often it happened that an obstacle would come and how quickly they would find a way to solve the problem and get on with the work—I just couldn't believe it. They were innovative and creative.

I didn't go out every two weeks to take an R&R like many folks did because it was too hard to leave and figure out what had happened while I was gone. It was just easier for me to stay. But, I remember one time I was up there three months and a week, and it was too long. I can remember getting up early in the morning and walking down the black rubber-striped halls to go to breakfast and looking at the floor and thinking, 'Am I going to do this forever? Is this ever going to end?' You get tired and stressed out.

The hardest for me was not having any exercise. They did, finally, build exercise rooms. But, I didn't go, because you had to go after dinner at night and I was always too tired. I missed the exercise terribly.

I remember the time there was a fire and how shocking it was how rapidly the module was totally consumed and how people barely got out. You wouldn't think you would have to exit so quickly if there was a fire, but with a furnace installed every four doors, you can see how fast a fire would spread with the pipes going around.

One time there was a fire in one of the camps and we had to take a bunch of the women into our camp. They came out panic-stricken and so thankful they were alive, with practically nothing but their nightgowns and maybe their shoes and a coat—nothing else.

Our training for exiting in case of a fire was to take a chair and break a window. Well, my window had snow and ice piled up to the top of it. I complained to the safety people and they had somebody come and just slice it out— like slicing a loaf of bread—so my window was exposed, and I could get out if I had to. It took me a while to realize

I was in jeopardy. The snow was thick, about six or seven feet out that way.

Comfort Food for the Mind

I bought big bottles of Lubriderm and everything else to take up there and put on my hands and my skin. It was terrible. That was hard. It was arid. It looked like there were piles and piles of snow, but it was just wind-drifted. It was very dry snow.

A lot of things were hard. It was hard to keep your spirits up after you'd been there for a while on one job. One nice thing I will always appreciate were the cooks and chefs. If you had to be up there at Christmas or Thanksgiving, they would really put themselves out and have a fabulous dinner. They would decorate beautifully, and sometimes they would have ice carvings and everything else to take your mind off the fact you weren't home. I really appreciated it; I'm sure everyone else did also.

I saw so many fascinating things up there; my life was totally different. There is no way to describe it. Living in a remote area, under hazardous conditions like that, it's different from being down here and coddled.

Encountering Polar Animals and Birds

I remember how thrilled I was to see my first polar bear, just from a distance. We had to take the ice road close to the ocean. Somebody had sighted the polar bear out on the ice. It looked more yellow than white.

One time there was this grizzly bear hanging around the job, not too far from camp, and we were warned to not get out of our pickup. A lot of people were getting out of their pickups and going very close to take pictures, which was very dangerous because it was out there eating and guarding its food. They told us we didn't know how fast a grizzly bear could travel. If it decides its food supply is threatened, it will charge. People were very foolish to get so close.

We watched the caribou migrating and watched the mothers standing on the side. Their calves would get behind, and you'd see them worriedly looking for their child way back. Quite a long time later, a little one would come along that would find her. They never walked, but kind of loped along. That was very moving to me.

Another fun thing was when we were driving from the camp and we passed by a big pingo where the foxes lived. In the spring, the babies were out. There would be three or four different holes all over where they had the various entrances. They were brown foxes, but they turned white in winter. They would hop out of one hole and into another one.

One time we saw a fox investigating a bird nest. I think a goose had a made a nest on an island surrounded by a little bit of water. The fox had eggs in his mouth, one in each side. We watched him mark the nest to keep the other foxes away. That was very interesting.

I remember I loved seeing the birds, the swans. There were so many varieties of birds. I loved seeing all the flowers that came out in the spring, when you thought nothing could ever grow there at all and suddenly here they were blooming. The flowers were beautiful.

The Prudhoe Bay Experience

When I first went to the Slope, it was for the experience. That's what I really wanted to go for—to see what it was like and have the experience of being in Prudhoe Bay and look at the pipeline being built and learning all I could about it. It was fascinating for me to learn about the gathering systems through which the oil finally goes to Valdez.

But, the money was great in the end. I was making the most money I had ever made. I hated to give it up. That was the incentive to return after the first few times I went up. Where else could you make money like that? The money I made then is what I'm using now. It was because I saved it and it kept growing and growing. I wouldn't have missed the experience for anything in the world. I was there for eight years."

After her years on the Slope, Norma retired to Washington, where she married Eugene Carter, her boss and the person responsible for her Prudhoe Bay job. After Eugene Carter passed away, Norma savored her memories and liked to talk about her Arctic experiences with her "Gene" and loved to talk about her working days on the North Slope. Norma died in Redmond, Washington, on September 13, 2002, at age 84.

DONNA FORD

When I first met Donna, I was eager to hear her story because I had never talked to a security guard. So, I could not wait to hear her interesting reflections. She walked and moved like someone who had weight training or practiced tai chi for years. She was balanced and centered. I suspected her perspective would be different from everyone else, and I was right.

With her unique, safety-focused point of view, Donna shed light on the prostitution and gambling parts of pipeline life, making these topics relevant.

Donna's recollections about the planned and unplanned parties and events were so detailed I was astonished she could remember them after so many years. She described how workers wore badges to designate their class and privileges, which I found incredulous. And even more difficult to believe was the implementation of Rule J, where men could not talk to women during the day unless it was about business.

—Carla Williams

Getting a Cop Job

"I was in the US Air Force at the time and had about two months before I was going to get out, and I really didn't know what I was going to do. I was going to become a state trooper, but I walked out of the polygraph because I didn't like the line of questions they were asking.

So, I was at the Cop Shop, which was at the time owned by a guy named Mike, who also had a security and bad-check operation in town. The Cop Shop was a place where you could buy weapons, uniforms, and stuff like that because there wasn't a whole lot of that available in Anchorage back in the late 1970s.

I walked in and he said, 'Are you looking for a job?' I said, 'Well, no, I'm not right now, but I probably will be in a couple of months.' And he asked, 'What do you do?' I told him I was an investigator in the Air Force. He said, 'How would you like to go on the Slope?' I didn't have any idea what the Slope was. I said, 'Slope what?'

And he says, 'It's up in the oil fields, you know—ARCO, SOHIO.' I didn't know a whole lot about the pipeline. I guess I just wasn't reading the papers or, by being in the military, I was sheltered or something.

He said, 'I just happen to need a female.' He went on to say, 'The "feds" tell me I have to hire another female, so if you want a job, you can have it.' I wasn't looking for one, but I said, 'Sure.' Then he started telling me about this job. At the time, I think I was making an average of six dollars an hour in the military.

'Ya, you'd be making fifteen dollars an hour,' he said. 'You'd be working eighty-four hours a week. It's a beautiful place and you won't have to pay for anything. Room and board and all your food—everything is provided for you.' The way he talked I thought I was going to Club Med or something. He told me what day to be at the airport and met me there.

It was the day after Mount St. Helens blew in 1980, May 19. So, I met him at the Anchorage airport and he told me to get on this plane, which was designated solely for the oil-field workers with ARCO. I was the only female on the plane that day, except for the flight attendants, and didn't know what I was getting into.

I got off the plane and it was just a gravel strip and these facility-like things looming in the distance. My first impression was that I had made a mistake. I thought, 'What am I doing here?' Because it was May, there was a little bit of snow on the ground; it was still kind of cold and all mud.

The plane landed and the stairs came down, and I got off the plane and was in three inches of mud. They didn't have the nice buses they have now, so they herded us onto this rickety old school bus and nobody was very friendly. It wasn't like there was a greeter there or tour guide saying, 'This way, new people!'

So, I went to PBOC [*Prudhoe Bay Operations Camp*], which is where they drop you off for ARCO. I walked in the front lobby and started looking around. The kiosk, which was the spark-shaped [*diamond-shaped ARCO logo*] desk and reception area, was in the main lobby and manned by an ARCO receptionist. She said, 'Can I help you?' I said, 'I don't know; I'm supposed to work for Security.'

She pointed to the guys over in the corner and said, 'Go see them.' Two guys standing there in uniforms told me I was in the wrong place. They didn't say, 'Hi, welcome to the group,' or anything. It was just, 'You're in the wrong place.'

'Guards don't stay here,' they said. 'They stay down in the construction camp.' I said, 'Okay, well, how do I get to the construction camp?' 'Just a minute,' they said. 'We'll call somebody.' They called another guard and then told me to go out there and get in the van.' So, I went outside and boarded a van. Cautiously, I was thinking: 'Where is this guy taking me?'

So, down the road I went, heading toward the Main Construction Camp [*MCC*]. Upon arrival at the front door, I got out of the van and walked into the metal building. These weren't the nice buildings they have now; it was just a bunch of ATCO trailers stuck together. It was called

Prime Camp—better known by the residents as 'Slime Camp.' Later they changed the name to Staff Camp.

I went in the front door. It was bleak and dark. PBOC was bright and everything was as Mike had described the way I would live. But, it wasn't that way at MCC where I would be living.

I finally got in contact with a sergeant. My uniforms, which were provided, were already up there but didn't fit. They were too big and too baggy, except for the pant legs, which were too tight because they were men's pants. They didn't have women's sizes at all.

All the security guys were in one special wing, and they had a special housekeeper who took care of them. Whoever was working security in the camp either on the night shift or day shift would wake up everybody and have juice and coffee waiting. This was a thing Security [*employees*] did for themselves. Well, I didn't get in that wing because it was all men.

It was only myself and two other gals who were female guards at the time. So, we were with all the women in the women's wing; there were ten other females living there. The guys all had day and night sleeping situations in the two bedrooms because there was a day shift and a night shift operation in Security. So, they would always have the room to themselves.

I think my first roommate was a gal who was a carpenter or something. Guys are different in that you can throw two guys together sharing a room and it's like no big deal. You throw two women together and it's like, 'I don't know you; I don't know what your habits are.' You wanted a little bit of privacy, but you weren't going to get it in a double-status room with a complete stranger!

But, I stayed with her for just about two months and then they put me in with another Security gal. They hired another female Security gal, so there were four of us. But, that was back in the days when 'Rule J' was enforced.

Issues with the Opposite Sex

'Rule J' was an ARCO regulation that stated no male could talk to any female except for business or during business hours. Men were not allowed to fraternize with women because of the problem with men and women working and living in the same camp.

At the start of these oil field camps, the men would go home to their wives and the wives would hear they were 'sleeping with all these women up there.' In order to keep peace with the wives, ARCO came out with Rule J to protect themselves. And Security had to enforce it. Today men and women live everywhere in the camp. Back then, there were always certain wings that were just for women and men were not allowed in that wing.

Back in the early days, a woman would face a situation where she would run into sexual harassment or the possibility of sexual harassment occurring. It was just an inconvenience she didn't think she had to deal with, along with the normal differences of a 'woman in a man's world.' After suffering enough, she would complain to Human Resources [HR]. Most small-contract companies did not have an HR, so she would contact ARCO or SOHIO for assistance. Not being used to this new situation, they would scratch their heads and get together.

This happened long before sexual harassment was a big thing. Usually, the answer was, 'What's a woman doing working up here anyway?'

Stop this Slope Foolishness and Get Married

If I heard it once, I heard it a thousand times: 'You should quit and give your job to a man who needs to support a family.' My comeback was always, 'Well, who is going to support me? I have to support myself.' Then they would say, 'Well, you should get married.' Then I'd say, 'I've been there, done that, and checked it off my list!'

It was a 'good ol' boy' syndrome. It always had been, and I don't think that will ever change. Federal laws have created a situation where they have to promote women. I think if those federal laws hadn't come along, they wouldn't have promoted women or even had them in the workplace at Prudhoe Bay. By the end of the eighties, a lot of women were promoted to management positions. That is not true today!

After the big layoffs in '85 and '86 through '92, there was a big push for women in management positions, but not anymore. They might promote a woman now and again as a supervisor, but they won't let her get too high in the management ranks. There was a time when a woman with experience and knowledge would go right to the top. ARCO, SOHIO, BP—they brought in all these women managers, but where are they today? They're not there.

The guys had it a lot nicer because of the women. A perfect example was about seven years ago, at Kuparuk, when they had a female pilot on the Otter. They never had a bathroom in the hangar at Kuparuk. So, when the guys needed to go to the bathroom, they either went out behind the hangar and did their thing or they had to take the shuttle across the pad and street to the Kuparuk Operations Center [*KOC*].

Julie, the female pilot, didn't have time in between some flights to run over to KOC, because it would delay the flights. She got them to put in a Porta-Potti at the hangar, which wasn't a big deal, but it made a world of difference. Then, pretty soon they got water out at the hangar. She's no longer a pilot, but the guys are still using that Porta-Potti and the water.

Many Ways to Take Advantage of Opportunities

I got called into the office one shift at about two o'clock in the morning to look after a drunk prostitute with about eighteen thousand dollars in cash in her purse, until we could take her to the flight in Deadhorse the next morning. She looked like she had a rough time. We couldn't figure out how long she'd been there, but it had been at least two weeks.

Sometimes personnel would provide money for flights into Deadhorse and someone would pick up the prostitute from her flight. She would travel from camp to camp to camp for as long as she could stay. That was back in the days when guys didn't go home very often; they stayed for six months, eight months, sometimes a year. Occasionally, they would go home for a weekend or a week, but they pretty much stayed at the Slope camps; that was their home.

The prostitute would go from room to room to room and would keep the day workers company during the night and the night workers during the day. The guys would bring her food from the dining hall and look after her.

The housekeepers were the ones who would let us know. There were a lot of things on that little sign when you entered the oil field that were illegal, but prostitution wasn't one of them. You couldn't have alcohol, you couldn't have guns, you couldn't have drugs, and you couldn't have cameras in some places. But nothing said anything about prostitution.

These 'Ladies of the Day and Night' weren't registered residents of the camp, so that was the only thing we could charge them for, but somebody would have to let us know they were there. We usually didn't find out until they had been there two or three weeks. The housekeeper would walk in on them and say, 'You are not supposed to be here.' All we could do was escort them off the field.

Poker, Anyone?

There used to be poker games in the camps every night in which the pots could reach anywhere from five thousand dollars to fifty thousand dollars. Most of the workers would get paid in cash; it was before direct deposit and all that stuff. Their companies would come up and pay them in cash, so these guys would have hellacious poker parties.

Gambling was illegal if we wanted to enforce it. We were told not to enforce it, because as long as they didn't get rowdy and it was just a friendly game, then it was considered recreational.

I can only remember one game that got rowdy. It was about a thirty-five-thousand-dollar pot. One guy thought the other guy was cheating, so there was a little yelling and pushing and shoving, but that was about it. All in all, it was pretty tame.

Actually, it was fascinating to watch. It was like the 'Wide World of Poker,' a game every night, with usually the same guys. One guy didn't always win, so the money kind of passed among them. In essence, it WAS like recreation! There was usually someone who was the banker and who would handle all the money and hand out the chips.

They always played with chips. They didn't play with real money, but there was always somebody who had the money. That was one thing—they weren't allowed to have big piles of money on the table. Sometimes Security would just stand there and watch them. It wasn't their official job or anything. In fact, sometimes we were informed if there was going to be a big game. So, if you wanted to make your presence known, you'd just walk through. Sometimes we were beneficial.

I think we are doing more service things now than we did then. There were so many people back then because it was major construction. Staff Camp held maybe 300 people and Prime Camp held 2,200 people, so we could have a total of 2,500 at MCC alone, and that wasn't even counting the ARCO people. I think PBOC could hold another 380 or something.

Union and Non-Union Tension

A lot of the people there were union members, which created more jobs. With the union contracts, if you had more than two people, you had to have a foreman and a driver. If you had a carpenter, you had to have an apprentice who carried the tools. So, that just created more jobs for everybody. We couldn't even change light bulbs because that was the electrician's job.

There were always two buses going to the airport—one for staff people and one driven by the Teamster for the union folks. There was always duplication because the union folks would not ride with a non-union bus driver. And the union bus drivers would not haul staff people. So, that necessitated two buses going to the same place, duplicating the same jobs. That went on until December 1985, when the union contract was completed. Then, the union's workers went away just like that and the non-union contractors came onboard.

The union folks had certain privileges people don't have now. Like the '798-ers,' the pipeline guys who built the pipelines all throughout the fields. There was one union in Oklahoma where they got all these '798-ers.' If one of them got into trouble and ARCO or SOHIO would try and fire them, they would just go to the oil companies and say, 'He's part of our union and if he goes, we all go.' So, those guys would get away with a lot more things because they needed to have this pipeline built, and there was nobody in the state of Alaska that could build that much pipe. They had to come from Texas or Oklahoma.

Those Rowdy '798-ers'

One night we had a couple of '798-ers' get into it with each other. They ended up pulling a sink out of the wall in one of the bathrooms and slugged a security guard, ripped his shirt, and tore off his tie. We wrote up a report on it, and, of course, they had to come in and repair the bathroom because water was going everywhere. But, nothing ever happened to those two guys because if one went home, they all went home. So, a lot of things were swept under the rug just to get the pipeline laid down. You just had to turn your head and not look.

It was amazing to me how much drinking actually went on, but people acted pretty much like adults. I think the unwritten rule among the union folks was: 'If you want to drink, that's your problem, but you had better be at work on time, give a full ten or twelve hours, and complete your full day's work.' As long as they could do that, it was allowed. Safety wasn't as big of an issue back then.

Proving Yourself

I had a lot of big brothers in my coworkers. When I first went up there, I was only thirty-two and pretty naive. Even though I'd been an investigator in the Air Force, I'd never been around rowdy and loud Slope workers. There were five security guards who took me under their wing and protected me—they were my armor. It took six months to prove myself. I had to learn to trust them and they had to learn to trust me. I couldn't cry at the drop of a hat and couldn't blush every time they told an off-color joke. I had to be one of the guys to fit in. After I proved I could do that, I got these five big brothers protecting my back.

Tools 'R' Us

In the early days of construction, the money barrel was unending. There was no bottom to the pit. It was all 'cost-plus' contracts [*all expenses paid plus a guaranteed profit percentage*], and they had absolutely no idea how much the pipeline was going to cost, because something this size had never been done before. So even though they tried to keep control of things, everybody knew there were no rules governing this type of contract.

You needed a new hammer? Well, go get one. You need a new set of wrenches? Just go get them. Nobody ever marked anything back then, so how did you know what belonged to ARCO or BP or was something personal brought to the job by the worker? Now they have a mark on all tools whether they are owned by ARCO/BP or an individual.

Back then, if somebody took a set of tools, it wasn't worth firing them, because they could just get more tools from the company store. If you try and take tools away from the Slope now that are used by anybody on the Slope, or are like anything used on the Slope, you must have a material exit pass. You have to prove the items are yours . . . laptops, any kind of tool, knives—the kitchen helpers are always bringing their knives back and forth.

They probably buried as much stuff in that landfill up there as they bought. Maybe not tools, but definitely materials. They didn't think about storing for the next job; they would just take the excess out and bury it because they knew they could buy brand new stuff for the next job.

Cowboy Roy

The person who stood out most to me was a production superintendent named Roy. He was one of the most down-to-earth good old boys and a real company man. There was a joke going around at ARCO that you would get issued a pickup truck and a secretary, because every one of the supervisors up there had his own truck and secretary. The joke with Roy was that his father was issued a horse and a secretary, because his dad worked for Sinclair back in the early 1900s, which eventually became Richfield and then Atlantic Richfield Company.

Roy started working for Richfield when he was sixteen, and he'd been working for them ever since. He was a good ol' boy with a heart, and I think what stood out the most was his cowboy boots. I used to give him a hard time about his boots. He must have had a dozen different pairs that he would think nothing of paying eight hundred to a thousand dollars for, but he wouldn't buy his wife a microwave.

I used to give him a hard time. I'd say, 'How much did those boots cost, Roy?' He'd say, 'I think they are ostrich and they cost six hundred dollars.' Then I'd say, 'Did you buy your wife that microwave yet?' He'd say, 'She don't need no microwave!' He thought it would make her lazy. If she had a microwave, she'd just quit cooking.

Five-Star Food

We used to have three steak nights a week. There was prime rib on Sunday, which is still served. On Tuesday, we would have T-bone steak, and on Thursday night, New York strip steaks were served. At least three nights a week, we had some other type of beef meal like stroganoff or stew. Once a week we used to have prawns or fried shrimp, but now we only have that for special occasions. We would have crab legs once a month, just because they were popular.

We have a lot more casseroles and chicken now. There was always meat and fish and alternative meat. There was always beef, pork chops, and fish.

Now you have one entrée and it's not necessarily beef. The 'Heart Smart' program started in 1987 or 1988. It was a big push all over corporate America to have exercise rooms and take more care about providing a healthier menu—more salad bars, less gravies, more dry stuff, and pastas.

It's not necessarily the food that gave the most calories; it was the pastries. It's so much easier to go into the spike room [*a 24-hour snack area*] and grab a cookie than it is to fix yourself something healthy. Everybody falls into the traps.

I don't know anyone who has gone up there and stayed longer than a year on the job who hasn't gained at least fifteen pounds—not one person. That is in spite of the fact that they now offer 'Heart Smart' food at every meal and there is exercise equipment of all types and levels. As they expanded the television channels, all I wanted to do was go to my room.

Zoning Out on Television

When I first went up there, they only had six hours of television programming provided by Channel 11 [*CBS*] from Anchorage that they showed four times a day. They did it on the drilling rig schedule because the drilling rig was the most important thing. So, it was noon to 6:00 p.m., 6:00 p.m. to midnight, midnight to 6:00 a.m., and 6:00 a.m. to noon. The tapes were shipped up on the plane, so they would just repeat that, and when the six hours were up, they would run it again.

Now, it varies, but we have thirty channels at Endicott. We have twenty-two channels at Kuparuk. ARCO Prudhoe has twenty and BP has about thirty—two or three movies channels and all the sports channels. So, it is easy to go back to your room, carrying your meal in a Styrofoam container. Since we weren't eating in the dining hall, I think the introduction of Styrofoam on the Slope hurt the socialization that went on up there.

I miss the fun back in the early days, the eighties. We used to have a heck of a lot of fun. You did your job and you worked hard at your job, but then you got to play. Every month we had some sort of a dance, whether it was just someone playing records and tapes, or a DJ was brought up from Anchorage.

Guest entertainers would come up, like Hobo Jim or Joanne & Monte. We had the Arctic Winter Games up there one year, right at the ARCO base camp. They came in and did their stuff and invited everyone to come try the ear pull and the knuckle walk (knuckle hop), so everybody got involved.

Party Hearty

Parties always had a theme, usually the theme of the month. There was a New Year's party in January, a Valentine's party in February, a St. Patrick's Day party in March, and in April you'd have an April Showers party, and in May you'd have the Maypole. Every month there was something fun going on that was paid for by ARCO.

There was a Little Theater and some of the employees would put on plays. Clara taught line dancing on several occasions. There were also athletic competitions like racquetball and softball tournaments. Softball was a big

thing in the summer and all the different contract companies had a team. They still have it, but it's not as big as it
used to be.

People aren't as dedicated—back then, they got shirts
and jackets from their teams just for playing. There are
no rewards now. The team who won the Top of the World
Softball Tournament got jackets, plaques, hats, and T-shirts.

Where Did You Get That Tan?

Two housekeepers used to get suntanned on top of one of
the ATCO units. They got some metal sheeting and made
a fort of sorts up there so they could go up on the roof after
they got off work and tan in their bathing suits. The sheet
metal would block the wind, and all they would get was
the heat from the sun.

Those gals had better tans than if they went to Hawaii
for two weeks—we were all jealous. They didn't look like
they had spent their whole summer on the North Slope.
Their job would require them to be on the Slope for eighteen or twenty weeks at a time, so that gave them a lot of
time to sunbathe. There were fire escape ladders to get up
on the roof on the side of the ATCO trailers. Nobody was
supposed to use them, but we thought it was ingenious
that they would think of it.

Silver and Gold Ingots for Some

I was fortunate to work for Security because the Security
contractors were like cousins to the oil company. Whatever
ARCO would give their people, like belt buckles, they always gave the same thing to Security. If they gave out gold
or silver ingots, we would always get them. Whenever the
oil company technicians got raises, Security got a raise.
Maybe it wasn't as much, but we were in their raise pattern.

After '85, they had the big layoff and the unions disappeared. That's when the oil companies divorced themselves from the contractors. This occurred because one of the contractors got laid off and filed a lawsuit saying he should get retirement from ARCO because he was treated like an ARCO employee. At the time, he lived in the same building as the ARCO employees, but his paychecks didn't come from ARCO, yet he got all the same benefits as the ARCO people did. In the eyes of the court, ARCO was a co-employer to this guy, so he won a retirement from ARCO.

From that time on, we had different mailboxes, we were no longer included in parties, and we were not included in the giveaways. It became 'us' and 'them.' It was almost like the people who had worked as contractors and got hired on by ARCO forgot who their friends were. One day they knew you, and the next day they couldn't talk to you because you were not ARCO; you were a contractor.

Brown, Yellow, and Red Stripes

The badges at Prudhoe caused a lot of it. The ARCO people had brown sparks on their badges. If you were a contractor who lived at PBOC, you had a brown stripe but no sparks. If you were a contractor who lived at MCC, you had a red stripe. If you did not live on the field at all but were allowed to come onto the field for business, you had a yellow stripe.

That started the whole class system. So, if you had sparks on your badge, you had total field access. If you had a brown stripe, you could go to most of the same places as the ARCO employees. If you had a red stripe, you could go wherever was needed for your job, but you didn't have free access to PBOC. If you had a yellow stripe, you could enter the field to conduct your business, but that was all. They still have badges and colors on the badges. The color defines your area of access.

One thing I liked about Kuparuk was there were no badges. Everybody wore the same blue coveralls. Some had APC [*Alaska Petroleum Contractors*] patches and some had ARCO sparks, but they all looked the same. They worked side-by-side. It was a smaller community and it worked very well.

A Rough, Tough Job for Women

I got a lot more respect than a lot of the gals did. Some of the gals got treated pretty rough, especially when they started coming up in 'crafts.' They were just apprentices. They got crap jobs, or the guys would leave them on the work site or make them clean the bus after lunch or whatever crap job they could find for the gals to complete.

On the opposite end, the supervisors who came up were issued a truck and a secretary. Those secretaries were pampered. It was mostly in the Projects Group. They were pampered 'ladies' because they worked for someone who was respected or needed by ARCO/BP, and a lot of those ended up marrying their bosses or causing a divorce between their boss and his wife.

Fuddy-Duddies

A lot of the young people coming up now are engineers—electrical, mechanical, and petroleum—and they are so focused on their job that they don't know when to turn it off. They have guys who will come in on Monday's flight and work fifteen hours a day until they go home the next Monday. They get the little take-out boxes for their lunch and go back to their offices and eat.

All in all, working on the slope was the BEST JOB I ever had. It paid well, took care of my every need, and gave me an opportunity to save for my retirement. This type of life-style was not for everyone, but those of us who maintained a good working relationship with each other and worked together to 'get the job done' achieved more than finan-cial gain. We gained lifelong friendships, experiences, and knowledge. I enjoyed MOST of the twenty-four years of service to the Alaska Oil Fields!"

Donna continued to work and enjoy her job on the Slope as a security officer until April 2004. At the time of this interview, she was working at Endicott.

DANA MARTINEZ PARKER

Dana was happy as she told me about her experiences in Alaska. I had worked with Dana and quickly discovered she brought a powerful presence into a room—everyone looked when she entered. She seemed unaware of her stunning beauty, but it was hard not to notice and stare. I could tell she loved her work by the way she described the "fun" of working on the North Slope. The people she worked with were special to her, and it was most likely very special for them to have her as a colleague.

Dana's background as a well operator, control board operator, and central processing facility manager was atypical for women working on the North Slope. Dana managed one of three central processing facilities supplying crude to the Trans-Alaska Pipeline at Kuparuk, the second-largest oil field in North America. The road to this responsibility was not easy.

—Carla Williams

Interview Hell

"When I first moved to Anchorage, they had full-page ads in the newspaper in 1985 seeking production operators on the Slope. That was when they were starting up Kuparuk. It was really difficult to get up there, not knowing anybody.

I kept interviewing over and over. I think I interviewed with Molly three or four times, and with all these other people, three or four times. We would come up as a gang, and then we'd get interviewed, and then Ernie would get the job. Then we'd all go back. Then we'd all come up again, and then Bob would get the job, and then it was like—okay, when will it be my turn?

I interviewed for two years for a Slope job—fourteen interviews. I didn't have my petroleum engineering degree, but I was close. There was always the preference for inhouse hiring, so I had that preference on my side, but had the downside of being a woman. It wasn't an easy thing, and it was a lot of who you knew. And, finally, in my case, it was what he said.

The reason I got my job was because one of the supervisors said, 'You'll never get a job up here; we have enough women.' The supervisor at CPF-1 [*Central Process ing Facility* 1] said, 'I don't know why you are interviewing up here; we've already got all the women we need. We've got our quota.' I went back and told my supervisor and he hit the roof. He said, 'They can't say that; they are not EVEN supposed to say that!'

So, he talked to the HR people and it blew up, and four days later the same guy was calling me to offer a job. He was saying things he shouldn't have been saying; that's why I mentioned it to my supervisor. It took a life of its own after I mentioned it, though. It was within only days I was offered a job. I think they would have been happy if I had been another guy that they could have gone fishing with, that being an additional criteria.

No Private Life

The key is to not take your private life up there. Nobody will come up and ask you directly about your personal life. That's one of the first things I noticed.

But the bullcooks, who are the housekeepers, know your life. Everything you have exposed in your room is there for them to see. I was in bed one night, thinking that I can't even turn in my bed without someone knowing about it. Also, like a high school thing—if you talk five extra minutes to one man, then they all are talking about it.

Shut-In All the Wells—Immediately

The worst thing that happened to me on the Slope was when a seawater tank didn't have a correctly sized vacuum breaker and the tank sucked in. Seawater injection was shutting down all the time, due to weather at the injection plant; they had just been down five or six times that week and it was not a problem. But, this time, due to pressure differentials, the boot, [*a flexible connection from the booster pumps to the turbine*] failed, so we had water flooding everywhere.

I was now in all this hell and chaos. We had the mechanics working on the booster-pump boot repair, and another operator came to my unit to assist in watching tank levels, since we were not pumping water. Due to a leaking valve, the operator assisted me in starting up the multiple turbines, collapsing the tank. We had to go 100-percent divert and close off all the inlet from the seawater. At that point, we shut the whole field down—almost. It was like . . . get as much water out of the system as possible.

I can remember standing up on the top deck overlooking the collapsed tank with the lead operator, looking across the whole field, and I was listening to my radio. And Rose, who had just started her new job on the control board, saying, 'Okay, can you shut-in wells Y23, 24, 25, 27, 22, 19, 13, 12?'—all the high-water producers. And, then, she would go to the next pad and say, 'Okay, now, can you shut-in this, this, this, and this, and then can you shut in this, this, this, and this . . . ?'

I was just standing there, thinking that all this oil production was in the dirt because this seawater tank was sucked in. I didn't push the button, but I was the operator in charge. It cost probably one hundred thousand barrels, at least. When you multiply that out, it's a hell of a mistake.

Up Bright and Early

We get up at four-thirty in the morning. We have to be at work at five-thirty or a quarter to six. The board operators work six in the morning to six at night.

You go to work, responsible for two drill sites, and you have this little routine, and then somebody says, 'Oh, by the way, could you come over here?' You are thinking to yourself, 'It's not on my list! It wasn't what I PLANNED on doing!'

I listen to the radio to see what's going on during my forty-five-minute drive to the drill site. I think it puts everybody in a foul mood if something goes wrong at the beginning of shift.

Major things only happen a couple of times a year, and when it's something major, I can't even think about the comfort of it; I just have to deal with it. It doesn't happen that often.

In fact, I can remember being assigned to drill sites the first two weeks thinking, 'When is something going to happen? I'm here; I'm ready!' Then the next week came, and I said to myself, 'I'm here; I'm ready. What's going to happen?' The next week would go by and it's like, 'Okay, I'M READY,' and then months would pass without a facility upset. Then you'd get this frantic call: 'Shut in ALL your wells!' or 'We just ESD'd [*emergency shutdown*] your skid!'

Manhandling

I don't manhandle anything anymore. I know when to back away. If there is somebody standing behind me who I know is much more qualified and can do the job and wants to help, I let him.

Early on, during the first couple of years, I never called for help. I would struggle. It would take forever, and I would do stupid things. But, there is that whole culture now—don't do stupid things. That's part of it, too.

There are a bunch of young guys out there lined up who want to have a part in the project. They don't like standing around. Who likes to just stand around? Everyone wants to play a part. I'll write out tags, and they close the valves. At least we are all feeling like we are part of the job. It's like . . . 'I'm going to be doing this, while you're doing that.'

But, you have to struggle; you have to do it yourself first. It depends on each person—how much struggling they are willing to put up with. There are people who struggle today who would never ask.

Equipment Likes It Cold

There is a point in the cold when you can no longer wear insulated boots; you have to go to bunnies [*bunny boots*]. That is just a fact of life. You just can't go out there with your regular boots at about minus twenty [*degrees Fahrenheit*].

At forty below, you just want to make sure you have enough fuel in your truck. And, you make sure the thermostat is one of those that runs hot, because keeping heat in your truck is one of your big worries. Lately, with the safety rules, at minus thirty-five, you don't have a lot of extra work going on. You just hold all outside work—anything that has to do with hydraulic or heavy equipment. The [*oil*] wells don't stop.

At forty below, your main concern is keeping everything going constant. When it's cold, turbines are running their best. The reality is when it's that cold, you are making the most oil you can. The operator's job is the worst in the summer because the board is always telling us to shut this in and shut that in, because of loss of turbine horsepower and the inability to process the gas. When it's freezing cold, everything is open. It always surprises me when equipment just runs and runs and runs. It's running right now. The equipment is designed to run thousands of hours before maintenance.

Stuck

When you are on the Slope, you're stuck there.

I can remember when I was working in oily waste and thinking it was the dreariest day . . . raining and muddy. I was looking out the window at the CPF and thinking, 'This is the dreariest place on earth. How did I end up here? Why am I here?'

But, then, the next day you can be doing something really exciting. You are 'ON' twelve hours a day.

When I first got up there, I'd have maybe two drill sites, and it was like—'Okay, I've got twelve hours to kill, and I have a lot of stuff I have to do that could be done fairly quickly.' Now, I have twice that many drill sites, and I am going all day long.

Fun on the Job

There is always good clean fun. I thought I was 'sandjetting' the hell out of secondary, and I was opening all the valves and sandjetting. John [*my coworker*] walks in and says, 'What are you doing?' I say, 'I'm sandjetting.'

I felt like I'd done a hell of a job. And he said, 'Your supply line is blocked in!' He loved to do that. And, I said, 'What do you mean?' So, he pointed up to it and I said, 'Oh, I knew that.' I hadn't sandjetted! I had opened the drain valves, but nothing was going on.

I've had the most fun with things like that because John is so deadpan. He'd look at you and say, 'You're no sand-jetter!' The guys would always run you to the edge."

———————————

Dana worked her way up the oil-field positions and recently retired as a production facility manager. She cooks, hikes, travels, volunteers, and manages her real estate in Arizona.

ONICE McCLAIN

When I interviewed Onice in Anchorage, it was her final trip home to the Lower 48. She had just retired from a long career on the North Slope a few days earlier, and she had a stopover in Anchorage to visit friends.

For many years, she traveled back and forth on her various rotations on the Slope, but now she antici-pated living a settled life. She was planning on living on her farm.

Onice's Slope days included helicopter trips out to the remote wilderness. When she came face-to-face with a grizzly bear, she did not follow conventional wisdom.

Most important, she played a large role in equal pay for equal work in a day when it was not the norm.

—Carla Williams

An Exciting Time

"On my first arrival at camp, I was scared. I had no idea what it was going to be like. I got there, and it was totally dark, with snow, ice. I wandered around and finally they found me this room. It was with a lady, probably in her fifties. The reason she didn't already have a roommate was because she was gay. Back in those days, that wasn't accepted. They kept me in that room and I stayed a while, but finally I asked to leave. It was 1974, at Galbraith Lake, right next to Pump Station 4. I was naive to camp life.

I worked for Bechtel as a secretary to a project man-ager for pipe inspection. I was like an administrative assistant. I did all the R&R schedules, stuff like that. The phone system was really bad. I would start calling the next camp until I would finally make contact. If I needed to call about plane reservations, I would call Bechtel in Fairbanks and the girls in the office would help. It was like an information-gathering center, which is what it amounted to for about six months.

Few Phones, One Fax, but Lots of Helicopter Rides

A lot of times we would have a shutdown because they wouldn't pass the welds on the pipe. It would be a frenzy to get the paperwork signed and back out with new specifications. We couldn't just call on the phone and there was only one fax machine, so it was hard. Sometimes we just had to get in the truck and go out to where the pipe was.

Alyeska was a lot 'looser' in those days. I could hop in a chopper and go from one camp to the other, so I got to see a lot by flying around. If the chopper was going to take someone from another camp or another location, if they had room, they would ask if I wanted to go for a ride. Many times I couldn't go, but sometimes I could go a couple times a week.

In the summer, we used to do a lot of hiking up in the mountains. The chopper would drop us off. There are a lot of caves in that area, around the Brooks Range. There were four of us who wanted to hike, and we always had to watch for bears, but we would take flares. We'd keep going back and investigating. We couldn't wait to get back up there the next day. If we had to walk back down, it was like a two-hour walk, so normally the chopper would stop to pick us up.

Closing the Camps

I moved from Galbraith to Toolik and from Toolik to Franklin Bluffs. I just kept moving up the pipeline. After that, Bechtel left the Slope, and I went to work for AIC

[*Alaska International Construction*]. I helped close all the camps, so I was there during the frenzy.

They were supposed to return everything to the tundra, but they left a lot of the gravel pads because they were going to use them for maintaining the pipeline. The buildings weren't removed until the last. Now they are all gone. I went down to Franklin Bluffs about six months ago, just for the drive, to see what it looked like. It's all changed. It looks like it probably should, except for the gravel pad.

I walked every morning. Even in the winter, we had the treadmills, so we could walk inside. In the spring, I always walked outside. One of the superintendents told me one time that I shouldn't walk without someone in a pickup to bear-watch. I thought he was teasing me, because I walked every day. I always walked out back toward the Sag River in Prudhoe Bay, right behind our camp.

One day I was walking and came within ten feet of a grizzly bear. He was looking at me, and I was looking at him. He was just standing there when I looked up. If I had walked another ten feet, I'd have been right in his face.

They had always told us, 'Do not run when you see a bear; just stand still.' That was part of the training. I could NOT stand still! I ran four or five blocks and up the stairs into the dispatcher's office. I was breathing real hard, and my eyes were probably bigger than saucers. I said, 'There's a grizzly; call Security!' The dispatcher never looked up and said, 'Next time you walk, walk out front, in case I have to fill out an accident report.'

After that, I went to the recreation room and walked until my nerves settled down. But later, if the guys knew I was going to walk, they'd make a circle with the truck to make sure everything was safe.

Tens of Thousands of Caribou and a Polar Bear Encounter

I had never seen a caribou migration before . . . it was like tens of thousands of caribou. I had to sit for hours in order to get across the road. It was unbelievable.

You can never imagine that many animals together. These were crossing at different areas up and down the road, and Security would come and wouldn't let you by while they were crossing. One day I waited three and one half hours and they just kept coming. I had never seen that large of a group. In the last few years, we've had muskox. They don't pay too much attention. I've seen them run along the pipeline.

One other experience was when Shawn [*a coworker*] and I were driving from BP, taking the back road over to Prudhoe, and we were driving up toward West Dock and there was a big polar bear along the side of the road. I was driving, and Shawn was sitting on the right-hand side. The bear was about fifty feet from the road, going the same way. Shawn kept saying, 'Don't make eye contact!' I said, 'I can't even make eye contact; I'm driving the pickup!' She was panicky, but it was a beautiful sight because the bear was just loping along. He was going about fifteen miles an hour, keeping up with us.

Every year at Endicott there was a family of swans. We would take pictures every time we could get close. There were a lot of ducks. Our window faced the Sag River, and many times there were bears playing. You could see the caribou grazing and geese, swans, and ducks. We could just look out our window and see some wildlife. That was nice.

Where the Sag River goes into the ocean, there are grayling [*a species of freshwater fish in the salmon family*]. They have airboats now, but a long time ago they didn't. Some of us who worked at ARCO would get our licenses and, after work, go down and fish, just to get out of camp. A lot of times we would fish out at West Dock for trout and grayling. Afterward, we would use the barbecue grill out back.

I was only at Kuparuk about six months; the rest of the time I was at Prudhoe. I've worked for several companies and at most of the camps. Through the years, you continue to get closer to people because you live with them. You are sisters; you are best friends.

There are not too many people who have been there the length of time I have. They come and go a lot. I worked twenty-three years without a break in employment. There are a couple of company men who work on the drilling rigs who have been there a long time also.

I loved my job. I liked what I was doing. After I went to the Slope, there was always a challenge. I was actually the first woman office manager that H. C. Price hired in its entire company, in the Lower 48 and up here, so it was a challenge to make sure I did the job the way they expected. So, I was never bored. If you have a job you dearly love, you can put up with a lot.

Twenty-Two Weeks, Seven Days a Week, without a Break

I have worked twenty-two weeks without a break. You get to the point where you are not aware of another life. You think the Slope is the only life.

Usually, I spent money on clothes and makeup, but not a lot. I never liked clothes that much; I'd just buy enough to get by on. I had an interest in real estate, so I was always making payments on land and houses. I invested wisely.

I mostly missed being with friends and family. You make a family on the Slope, but I missed having a home life. I don't think I can ever make up for it; it's lost forever.

I would like to start now doing some of the things I missed, like family holidays, having my niece or nephew on Sunday or Saturday. There never was enough time to do all that. I missed seeing them grow up, their football and basketball games and stuff like that. I'm going back to school—cooking school. I'm a gourmet cook, and I've taken a lot of classes, but I'd like to take more.

Equal Pay for Equal Work

When you worked in administration or in the office, they would try to pay you less than a man in an administrative position. When I hired on, the other office managers, who were men, made more than I did. I think it was kind of a test to see if I could do the job. After they hired me, then they started hiring other women. I was never very scared to speak up, so I wouldn't let them get by with much, without letting them know. If they gave a man a raise, I would go in and say, 'Hey, I've got girls out there doing the same job!'

Working on bids was very involved. Trying to put together a bid so we could stay in business was very crucial. I would work all night, all day, several days in a row. I did all the typing and putting the bids together.

We'd crunch numbers and put it all on paper. Our first computer was an Apple, and the whole office used the one computer. I was amazed we ever got anything out of it. Sometimes we would work all night typing cost reports for the client.

Cocaine, Marijuana, and Liquor

Things changed a lot the first ten years on the Slope. It was wild, and a lot of things were going on. You could never go into a room without seeing cocaine or marijuana or beer or whiskey or whatever. Now you could never go into a room and find anything! It's just not there. I think that was a big change and a change for the best.

For a long while, I wouldn't go into a room because I would not have wanted it said I was in the same room where they had cocaine. If they were terminated, then they might say, 'Well, Onice was there. Why aren't you terminating her?' I just never wanted that stigma attached to my name.

I think the attitude has changed a lot now. I think people find their jobs are more important to them. It's a job; it's not a party.

Twenty years ago, you would buy the things that you would never buy; now it's a job. You have a family and you are trying to support them on a three-week-on, three-week-off job. People who are on a regular schedule don't make all that much money. It is more money than they can make in the Lower 48, but it's not all that much after taxes, so it's more like a normal job.

Four- to Five-Thousand-Dollar Weekly Paychecks

The oil companies tightened their belts once they got the pipeline in and all the construction done. I think they realized, to continue with their profits, they had to cut costs, so a lot of the wages went down.

It was nothing to see a four- to five-thousand-a-week paycheck during the pipeline. Our employees could draw up to two thousand dollars a week in cash from their paychecks. From the home office, our draw money was about fifty thousand dollars. They spent it on gambling, drugs, alcohol, and women.

They still gamble, but you don't see the big pots—just dollars or five dollars. They still have a lot of football pots for ten dollars—not the big ones, which were one hundred dollars a block."

———————————

Onice retired from the Slope in 2000 and lives on twenty acres of a 250-acre ranch in the Lower 48 with her older sister. The produce they raise keeps vegetables on the table all year. They have a variety of animals, including miniature donkeys. She frequently entertains and has horseshoe pits and dance floors for parties. She spends a lot of time with her relatives.

MARLENE McCARTY

Marlene traveled the United States as a Lady Shriner for many years and still does. She was a past Grand High Priestess of the Oriental Shrine of North America, which allowed her to crisscross America. She loves her current position as a retired snowbird living in Oregon most of the year. But she spends her summers in Alaska, where she has a home in Anchorage and one on the Kenai River.

Marlene talked about how being part of an oil-field family not only helped catapult her career, but also gave her a sense she had to work even harder for success. Her father, Eugene "Irish" Carter, was one of the early pioneer contractors on the North Slope and Kenai Peninsula near Anchorage. Her father owned, and Marlene and her brother helped manage, National Mechanical Contractors, Inc., where Marlene honed her management skills.

One year Marlene only had three weeks of R&R and begged her father for a day to fly into town just to shop. Marlene explained how others felt about her, how the young men handled the isolation and cold, and how whiteouts scared even the toughest men.

In her stories, the North Slope was not a place for the faint of heart. Marlene had many positions throughout her North Slope career, from purchasing agent to construction company manager. She spent many years as a materials coordinator, ensuring project materials were ordered and accessible for the construction crews.

—Carla Williams

Paying for a Job

"It was the July Fourth weekend, 1975. I went up to Prudhoe Bay to take my nephew Kenny, who was seven years old, to see his dad—my brother. I had brought him up to Anchorage from Seattle, and my father was going to go up to the Slope with us, but then he got called back to Seattle. Kenny, my nephew, and I got on the plane and went to Prudhoe Bay together.

I remember the first thing I saw when I got to Prudhoe was half of an airplane sitting right next to the terminal building. There had been a cargo plane that had split in two on the landing and they had left half the airplane sitting there. They had already hauled the tail section away, but that had been weeks before. It eventually ended up in Childs's (the Childs family was famous for salvage) junkyard.

The camp was very crowded. They put a bed in one of the offices for me. Kenny slept with his dad. It was called the Atwood Camp. It was later sold to NANA and called NANA Camp. It was right by the airport. We were there for just three days, then I went back up within a month and went to work.

I went with another gal, Patty. She was hired as a secretary, and I was a timekeeper for National Mechanical Contractors. At that time, they had to hire two women because the housing was so tight they could fill the room with two beds. They couldn't afford to bring just one woman. So, we were the only women in camp for a short time and then there were other Teamsters. We put the pilings in, and we were building the ARCO construction camp at that time, the Prime Camp.

We had a contract to refurbish the Texoma drills for ARCO, and then we were putting in these pilings. We were drilling holes in the tundra for the pilings for buildings and for structural support for the pipeline. I was working in the office. We were a subcontractor under Parsons, the engineering firm and managing general contractor for ARCO.

Then I joined the Teamsters Union because through the refurbishing of these Texomas, I was ordering parts. The Teamsters harassed the mechanics and said we had to have a Teamster; it was a jurisdictional thing. So, I called my dad and said I wanted to get in the Teamsters Union and he needed to hire me in this position. He said, 'Okay, let me make a phone call.' He called me back and said to send three hundred dollars to Cal [*union representative*]. That's how I joined the Teamsters.

Facing Off with the Guys

They sent my dispatch to the field. I moved my office out to the shop and started being a parts person. I had an advantage up there because my dad and brother were running the company [*National Mechanical Contractors*]. I wasn't harassed. If anyone knew who I was, they would try to say things to me.

Being a daughter of management, I had another problem—I had to prove myself to the guy who was our general manager at the time—Jack—who didn't want me there. He was trying to get rid of me, so I had a problem with him.

I finally told him he wasn't working for the telephone company. He was working for Irish Carter and he could piss me off all he wanted to, but I wasn't going to leave. I said he probably couldn't get my dad to fire me, so he probably had better start getting along. So, he backed down. Besides, he had two of his kids working for the company, too.

The master mechanic who I worked for was a grizzly, old, outspoken guy who got me in the truck the first day I worked for him. He said, 'There are two things I want you to know. The Teamsters got some rule that if you got three people in a truck, you got to have a Teamster driver.'

Then he said, 'This is my truck and I'll drive it no matter how many people I've got in it! The other thing I want you to know is how I feel about you people. If you back up and you hit a bump and you hear broken glass and smell shit, you probably ran over a Teamster with glasses on!'

So, he really didn't have much use for my trade. Not only that, but I was a woman invading his shop.

Of course, they had the usual beaver shots of women on the walls. They papered the walls with them. At that time, the people who sold tools and equipment put out girlie posters and they were all like the centerfolds or worse. They had to take down all those things because my father insisted I didn't have to work in an office where I had to look at that. That made the guys mad, but they grew to love me. They were like brothers.

You become part of the family. Up there, what happens is you are working with people twenty-four hours a day, and anybody who is phony just doesn't cut it, because it becomes evident so quickly. It is such a microcosm of humanity in one small place. You know too much about each other in many cases. The hard thing is to distance yourself from other people's problems. Good people rise to the surface and the others become very evident right away.

Opportunity to Leave the Slope

We worked very long hitches then—nine weeks on and two weeks off, supposedly. When we had the maintenance contract with ARCO, in one year I had a total of three weeks off. I called Dad in Anchorage for time off and he said, 'The job's not over!' Then I said, 'It's a three-year maintenance contract—I can't live that long!' He said,

'What's the matter—are you in love? What do you need to come to town for? Whatever you need, we will send it to you.' I told him I just needed to get out of there and see neon lights, pregnant women, old folks, children, dogs, and things they didn't have there, like shopping.

After that first hitch, I came to the Anchorage office for a little while. In November of that year, I went to Fairbanks. We had to deal with all the unions in Fairbanks and our office was in Anchorage, so Dad sent me to Fairbanks to be the dispatcher and run parts for the drilling operation that was going on there.

I dispatched all the people. When they came to me, I'd put them through their Arctic training at Fort Wainwright and get them geared up with all their Arctic gear and send them to the Slope. We did all this through Parsons. They paid the tickets, but I had to get vouchers from them and would meet the 798 [*union*] welders who would come in from the Lower 48.

They would get off the airplane in Fairbanks in a polyester jumpsuit and a pair of pointy-toed boots and a cowboy hat, and 20 percent of them would just turn around and get a ticket home. It was cold, and they weren't staying. For the ones who stayed, I would keep a couple of old parkas in my truck, and if they didn't have a decent coat, I'd give them one until I could get them geared up.

Whiteouts and Homesickness

In the first week of December, they had a whiteout situation in Fairbanks that lasted for eleven or thirteen days, where it was sixty-five below and no airplanes flying. A trip that would normally take forty minutes took almost four hours.

The snow up there is very dry, and it blows around like a sandstorm. It's like being in a desert sandstorm. There is no horizon, nothing. People tell stories about having to go out and feel, by hand, for the road or have somebody walk it in front of the headlights.

In the meantime, some guys came in and I couldn't get them out of town; the flights were not going. They were all housed at the Polaris Hotel, and I'd have to go down every morning and 're-voucher' for the next day. I'd either take them to the airport or get them transportation to the airport in case the flight did happen. That went on for days.

A lot of them were young kids who had never been away from home before, let alone Oklahoma or wherever they were from. They were coming up here as helpers and they were in trouble with the hookers or trouble with the booze; it was a real circus. It was a wild town, Fairbanks was, in those days.

They issued gear at Alyeska and had cold weather training at the base. They would submit a voucher with how much they had spent, and we would deduct the amount from their paycheck.

Frozen in the Snow

I can remember a guy dying up there. We had a man working for us who had been supervising a night crew for ARCO. He also worked during the day. He had a foreman on the night shift, but he would go out and check on him.

The supervisor didn't show up for work one morning. Everybody thought he had worked late the night before. They didn't want to wake up the night crew—they had already gone to bed, but they couldn't find anyone who had actually seen him. They started getting antsy, so they went and talked to the bullcook, the person who made up his bed, and she said he hadn't slept in his bed all night. He wasn't out at the work site. They finally got the foreman out of bed, and he hadn't seen him out there the whole shift, so we were all looking for him.

The last time anybody had seen him was leaving the dining room, then walking from the dining room at Staff Camp down to the offices at the end of the hallway. Somebody had passed him in the hallway. We went out and found him; he had had a heart attack and collapsed by his truck. Apparently, he had gone out there to plug in his truck and the snow had covered him up because it had blown hard that night.

At that time, they didn't have any caskets. So, our carpenter made a wooden box. They put him into this casket and put him in the back of my truck. I drove him to Alaska Airlines and parked the truck at the airport. It was sad for anyone to die like that and so far away from home. As it turned out later, he had a history of problems we didn't know about and probably shouldn't have been up there.

Fun and Entertainment

The Prudhoe Bay Follies would put on these fabulous shows and everyone would volunteer his or her talent. They would say, 'I can't sing,' or 'I can't dance,' or 'I can't this and I can't do that.' Then, once you got them on the stage, you couldn't get them off! People just loved it.

There were 'Saturday Night Live' takeoffs, like the 'Killer Bees,' funny skits, and musical numbers. The ingenuity of people to throw a party was really something. Getting the refreshments in was always a challenge. Everybody blamed the truckers for bringing it in, but there were numerous ways people knew how to smuggle things in.

I can remember twenty cases [*of alcohol*] coming inside the bucket of a loader. The guy went in and out of the checkpoint all the time and just had the bucket up high enough above the security guard's vision when he carried it through. We used to stash it on the top shelf of the warehouse, inside the floors and walls; carpenters could do anything.

Advances to Women

Certainly, there were those of us who helped each other. Women who worked for other companies who were getting harassed by their bosses, pipefitters, laborers, and bullcooks would say, 'What can I do?' If it was somebody who worked for us, I could do something directly. I could threaten their livelihood if they didn't cease and desist.

I didn't have a lot of tact. I just went to them and told them that maybe they would like to have pictures sent to their wife or maybe I could just call their business agent. It was all about power. A foreman had power over the people working for him, and if it was a female he wanted to request favors from, some of them didn't worry about doing it. They weren't the majority and most of the guys were pretty decent, but there were some bad apples.

I did have an incident up there where something got out of hand. When they went to having Sundays off, people didn't have anything to do on Sundays. A lot of people who could have worked would get on the airplane, and, if they lived in Fairbanks, they would go home Saturday after shift and be back Sunday. People who lived outside or couldn't afford it would stay.

With our maintenance contract, we had to keep one person from each trade around, but most people would do their laundry and then they had nothing else to do. If the weather was decent, they would take the truck and run down the haul road, since that was the only direction they could go.

This guy invited this girl to take a ride down the high-way and there was alcohol involved. He started to make advances that weren't being reciprocated, and she ended up getting out of the truck and running down the haul road and flagging down a trucker, who brought her back to camp. We had a female state trooper up there. He had to stand trial. He didn't do any bodily harm; didn't rape her. It hadn't gone that far.

I was in the middle of it because I was the supervisor. He ended up leaving the Slope and she stayed. When we brought him back as an employee, we had to house him off-campus in another camp. That was his penalty. It got sticky and there were a lot of statements. I was never called to court, but I think the women who worked in the crafts had it rough unless they had a mentor.

Cohabitation Challenges

I ended up at NANA Camp in Prudhoe Bay with 250 men, but I got lonesome for the sound of a female voice. Men just aren't interested in some of the things we [*women*] want to talk about or need to talk about. Sometimes we just needed to get things off our chest.

You always had a roommate when the camp was full. There were any number of ingenious ways to get a single-status room so you could have company. The easiest was getting booked in with someone who worked nights. Or there would be two gals who would room together and two guys, but they were cohabitating. The names on the doors said Jack and John and Mary and Sue, but, really, it was Jack and Mary and Sue and John, and everybody knew it.

Security knew everything that was going on there. They didn't have anything else to do but watch. They couldn't allow anyone to cohabitate if they weren't married. They didn't want to see a marriage license; they just wanted someone else to take the responsibility to say they were married. So, if your project manager or supervisor wrote a letter that said, 'This is to authorize so-and-so, who are husband and wife, to occupy the same room,' they would send it to ARCO and nobody questioned it.

They didn't do that at BP. As far as I know, all the years I lived there, BP never allowed it, but ARCO did allow living together. And there were legitimate married couples, people who had real marriage licenses, who lived together.

In 1975, during the time I was there, they locked up the women's wing, just like we were criminals. They took the door handles off the outside of the doors, so you couldn't get in from the exterior. You could get out with the crash bar, but not in.

They also patrolled the hallway at the other end when you went into the main hall. Someone would be right there watching when you went in and out of the room. It wasn't that the guys couldn't go in the wing at all; it was that they were supposed to be out of there by ten o'clock at night. It was like a college dorm, but few people up there were under twenty years of age.

One night they found a bunch of guys in the women's wing. I wasn't there because I was sleeping over at NANA Camp. They took all the women out of the rooms and locked them in the infirmary—all of them—not just the two women who had guys in the room. That was a gestapo act as far as I was concerned. Can you imagine getting routed out of your bed and taken to the infirmary and locked in?

Movie and Television Reels

The thing that has changed for the better is television, and that came early. Alaska had one of the first satellites and ARCO had the first one up there. That probably cut down on the alcohol consumption and a lot of other problems. Now people go to their rooms and don't wander the hallways.

Back then, eight-track cassettes and movies were shipped in. Movie reels came in from Anchorage and we shared them, going from camp to camp. A lot of the movies shown in the camp weren't movies I wanted to see; the guys did, but I didn't want to see them because they made me feel uncomfortable. They still run movies at camp, but I think they are three or four nights a week, not every night. Communication is better now and there is more diversity. There are women engineers, so that's changed.

Computers—of course, we didn't have those then. I went to Seattle and talked to IBM and we had a computer payroll system in 1976. We had a fax machine in 1975; I faxed my orders to Bill in Anchorage—it was the old thermo-paper. It wasn't fast, but it was better than talking to him on the phone for an hour or more.

We were probably doing a lot more than we thought we were at the time. We set up a computer system in the Seattle office. Now when I go up there, I have less responsibility and less worries. With everyone having faxes and computers, my job is much easier. The methods for shipments are better. They have better carrier facilities now up there. They take better care environmentally.

Reunions

I still see people who I knew from way back, but most of them were apprentices and now they are bosses. We talked about having a Pioneers Home [*retirement facility for early Alaska pioneers*] up there. Nobody wants to live there all the time, but we want to go back and visit our friends. I guess we will have to have reunions. You take a bunch of people, all doing the same thing, at the same time, in the same situation, and they get together in small rooms and build friendships. I was fortunate that my brother and dad were there, but most didn't have family. It seems since I've left, most of my friends are related to construction and the Slope."

––––––––––––––

No grass grows under Marlene's feet. She appears to others as a non-stop traveler. Her brother Pete, nephew Kenny, and father Eugene, all of whom she mentions in her interview, have passed away, but she has many nieces, nephews, and friends who rely on her visits and attention. Marlene is happily retired in Oregon after a lifetime of working in the oil fields of Alaska. She spends her summers in Alaska.

ROXIE (HOLLINGSWORTH) MAJESKE

I first met Roxie on the North Slope. She was guiding a group through a drill site and explaining the operation. I thought of Roxie as a role model, no matter what the profession. I jumped at the chance to interview her and was thrilled she accepted.

Roxie talked about what it was like to work on a wireline unit, which is working on the actual oil-well holes. This is dangerous work involving high-pressure wells, and mistakes could mean serious injuries or death. Oil wells are on land and on islands, with small living quarters. Roxie is a tough woman and it shows in this interview.

—Carla Williams

Flat as a Pancake

"The first thing I thought about when I got there was how flat it was; no trees, nothing. I had gone to the Seward Skill Center. They had an eight-month-long course but had just shortened it to four months. It was called Roughneck Development. I just wanted to do something to get on the Slope, so I signed up, but it took almost two years to get enrolled.

I wanted to go to work on a drilling rig as a floor hand, as a roughneck. So, right when the school was almost over, Otis Engineering, the wireline company, gave them four applications and said they would guarantee interviews to four people, but I didn't want to work for them. I graduated from the course and went banging on doors trying to get on a rig.

After I did that for about two months, I decided that since Otis was offering the interview, I would go do that and they ended up hiring me. They do 'downhole' work—the wireline unit. They go in after they have already drilled. When I was in high school, I wanted to work on the pipeline. My two dreams were to go to work on the pipeline and to build a cabin out in the middle of nowhere.

Working "Downhole"

My very first job with Otis was on a drilling rig. Our wireline unit went out to the drilling rig and we were there all night long. The sun was up all night, which was really neat. The longest I remember working at one time was forty hours, but we did quite a few jobs that were not much less than forty hours. I just went out and worked until the job was done.

My first day I was up all night long. We went out to the drilling rig, rigged up, and we were on the rig all night and into the next day. One of my first thoughts then was that I was thankful I was working on a wireline unit and not on the actual drilling rig. It was kind of scary going to work on rigs. It seemed dangerous and they didn't treat people very well. They were tough on anybody who came on their rig; they would try and scare them. As a woman, it was intimidating being there. I would have to let them know I was not scared or they would just feed on it.

I had worked six months on 'slickline'; then they wanted me to work on 'E-line.' Slickline does mainly downhole repair work. E-line has the conductor and they do different types of monitoring.

On E-line, you work with smaller well-servicing equipment and you go out and rig up. You stay rigged up a lot longer than slickline. On slickline, you would rig up

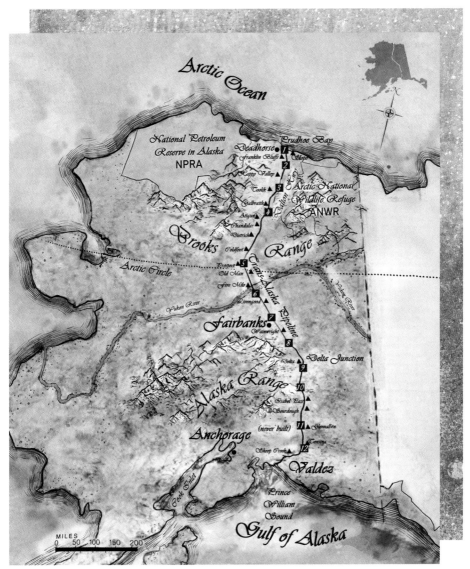

Map of the pump stations and pipeline camps. BY JULIA FEUER-COTTER

Caribou near well pad with pipeline in the distance. BY CARLA WILLIAMS

Carla Williams in front of crew cab at forty below zero. BY CARLA WILLIAMS

Carla Williams inside wellhead shelter next to wellhead. BY CARLA WILLIAMS

Stab-in and bolting vertical support members (VSMs) for pipeline. BY DEBORA STRUTZ

Sisters Mable Rockstad (right) and Betty Sevlin (left) inside the Trans-Alaska Pipeline near Delta Junction in 1976. BY LIANNE ROCKSTAD

Lianne Rockstad in 2017.
BY BRIAN WALKER

Debora Strutz with the bus she drove from camp to the field worksites. BY DEBORA STRUTZ

Alpine safety stickmen, which introduced fun into a safety message. BY DEBORA STRUTZ

Norma Smith in her office at Prudhoe Bay in the early 1980s.
BY NORMA SMITH

Dana Martinez Parker turning valve at Kuparuk. BY DANA MARTINEZ PARKER

Large diameter pipes called flow lines coming from a well pad. BY CARLA WILLIAMS

Dana Martinez Parker (left) and Carla Williams (right) in front of a wellhead shelter.
BY CARLA WILLIAMS

Marlene McCarty at Prudhoe Bay. BY MARLENE MCCARTY

Erecting a snow fence to catch drifting snow at Prudhoe Bay. BY DEBORA STRUTZ

Typical North Slope mobile drilling rig, several stories high, which moves from pad to pad via the dirt roads. BY GRETA ARTMAN

A recent photo of Kate Cotten. PHOTO COURTESY OF THERESA LEAH KUHEL.

Samantha George in front of electrical junction boxes at Kuparuk in about 2014.
BY SAMANTHA GEORGE

Samantha George overlooking flow lines and Arctic tundra while standing on a divert tank.
BY SAMANTHA GEORGE

Gwen (Skeet) Sloan at her desk in the 1970s. BY GRETA ARTMAN

Pipeline monument by Malcolm Alexander at the pipeline terminal in Valdez. BY B.N.M. PRODUCTIONS

Pipeline construction worker Linda Templeton leans on a shovel. ALASKA STATE LIBRARY, HISTORICAL COLLECTIONS, PIPELINE IMPACT PHOTOGRAPH COLLECTION, 1974-1977. ASL-PCA-17. (ASL-P17-8034).

and down, sometimes four or five times a day—depending upon what was going on—with a lot bigger equipment, bigger tools. So, E-line was easier.

There were several people who were pushing me to break out as an operator, actually run the unit. The guy who was the supervisor for slickline didn't want me to leave; he wanted me to stay in the slickline department. So, it didn't take very long, and I had several people who were pulling for me to make it.

When I first went to the Slope with Otis, there were a bunch of guys who did not want women there because there weren't any other women who worked in any type of wireline work up there. I was the first female wireliner on the Slope. This was before Kuparuk. There have been a couple women since then.

You had to be strong. Knowing what I know now, I would never do that again, because I pushed myself constantly. I did what everybody else did. I didn't ever let it stop me that I was a woman. I just jumped right in there and gave it my all. And, I could do it, but I think that years down the road you pay the price. I've been on the Slope since July of 1981. I swapped weeks a couple of times, but other than that, just one week on and one week off.

Working on the Arctic Ocean

Some of the interesting jobs were in the wintertime when the sea would freeze up and we would go out on a man-made island. There would be drilling rigs out there doing exploratory work and we would go out and do different jobs on them. I've worked on rigs that won't even tell you what they are doing there.

Being way out there on the ice, that was interesting. On one rig job, I got out there and we were going to stay the whole week, so they assigned us all rooms in the rig camp.

Since they had so many people, they had this barge that they had a couple ATCO trailers on. It was kind of tipped up on the island and frozen-in like that, and I was supposed to room in one of those rooms.

I walked over there, and it was tilted, and there were four doors on the outside of this trailer, which meant four different rooms. I opened the door from the outside and I was in the room. Guys had been peeing right outside the door. I opened the door that I was supposed to stay in and there was some guy sleeping, and I just shut the door and thought, 'No way!'

I just went over to where the rest of the guys on my crew were and we rotated through the room. It was like . . . 'I don't need my own room.' I had to deal with things like that a lot. At times, there would not be a women's bathroom I could use. I would just have to use the men's and some guys didn't like that a bit. You'd just go in and keep your eyes straight and go right to the bathroom.

Pop the Lubricator

In the wintertime, we wore Refrigiwear and Green Ape gloves, which are just cotton gloves. It was hard to keep our hands warm. But you needed to be able to move your hands to do things; you were outside rigging up. The colder it got, the less you could work outside, so you would go outside for as long as you could, and you would go inside and warm up and then back outside as soon as you were warm.

If the job was a long one, there were bunks in the unit and you just laid down and took a nap whenever you could. There wasn't very much room on a wireline unit. There used to be two bunks on them. While the operator was running in the hole, you would lie down and sleep for fifteen minutes, maybe an hour, if you were lucky. At that time, I did just fine with it. It was expected of you and you didn't think any different.

Things have changed a lot from when I first went up. Now, I think they are a lot more safety conscious. I went up almost eighteen years ago. Before, when I worked for Otis, it was pretty much just rush, rush, rush; get the job done. If the operator was almost out of the hole and you weren't out the door ready to pop the lubricator and change tools, he was yelling at you. It was hard-core. Now they really stress safety; they want you to stop and think about it. At the time, that was just the way it was, and you didn't know any different.

Tools in the Hole

They have better systems for maintaining pressure control, such as a shield around the top of the lubricator and a little drip basin underneath it.

I've never left a tool in the hole. If you do, you fish it out. It's not that big of a deal, unless there is a big mess of wire or maybe you broke a tool or there are pieces of a tool around your tool's string. Then, you can have a lot of problems, but if you've got just a tool string and a little wire, all you do is drop a tool down and clip that wire off and get the wire out and go down and latch on to the tool string. It can be an easy thing, or it can create a work over; it just depends upon the situation.

Start-Up

I remember one year they decided they weren't going to have a cutoff temperature [*when work stops due to cold*] for us and it seemed like it was colder that winter than any winter. We just worked no matter what temperature.

When I first went up there, they didn't have platforms on a lot of the wellheads. The wellheads in Prudhoe are a lot bigger than the ones in Kuparuk, and you had to climb it. You would climb the wellhead hanging onto the nuts and bolts and just get up there and sit on something. The big BOPs [*blowout preventers*] and lubricators [*contain well pressure while wireline is going in and out*] would swing at you and you'd have to grab it and stab it on.

Some of the 'trees' at Prudhoe are up to thirty feet tall. I climbed up and hung on and I was always dirtier than everybody else because I wrapped myself around it.

You can lose your pressure control. Like on E-line, you have a grease head that maintains your wellhead and pressure control and you pump grease in up to the top. There are some rubber seals and just the combination of the seals and the right consistency of grease, depending upon the temperature, is what maintains the pressure. You can lose that and be blowing gas or oil out the top; then, you work at trying to get that seal back.

It's scary. It's a horrible feeling in your stomach because you just don't want that to happen. You say, 'Oh shit!' When it was E-line, you had a stripper you could hydraulically pump up and close the rubber seal in around your wire. You might possibly have to change grease, and your temperatures might be fluctuating, and you might have the wrong consistency of grease for that temperature. So, you have a big drum of grease that you pull out and put a new one in. [*Heat socks are also used to warm the grease.*]

Polar Bear Sighting

In the summer, the whole place just comes to life. Near the drill sites, snowy owls hang out in the summertime. You get to see baby swans and watch them growing up before they take off in the fall.

I saw my first polar bear last year. It was just as impressive as I knew it would be. He was moving, and I saw him from a side view; it was like slow motion. It was just as it was getting daylight in the morning, so it was a neat background. He was probably one hundred yards away and I was in my truck. I would have just taken off quickly if I needed to, but he just kept walking. Later that day he was hanging out on some ice, just lounging around.

Two Christmases

Since I'm a mom, I have a tough time leaving my son. He's going to be five years old and starting school, then he's going to be ten years old, then fifteen years old, and then he's going to be gone.

I'm up there for a full week, but by the time I get home, I'm constantly in a state of preparing to leave again. Luckily, since my son has been born, I've got Christmas off. This year, for the first time since he has been born, I'm going to be working on his birthday, but I'm taking three weeks off right after that when he starts school.

You get used to working holidays. In the past, my family would celebrate Christmas either before or after. When my oldest brother started having kids, they would have two Christmases because they would have Christmas on Christmas Day and then the big Christmas when I was home. My youngest brother is working up there now. He drives cat for a cat train."

––––––––––––––––––

At the time of the interview, Roxie worked on the Slope as a drill site operator. Drill site operators oversee one to several drill sites and ensure the correct people are on-site at any one time. They monitor people coming and going onto the site and manage any issue that arises at the drill sites.

The drill site operators physically open and close valves by hand in some cases, sometimes high off the ground, which requires climbing around on platforms, rails, and scaffolding. They are in radio contact with the control board operators at all times, in case something needs to occur rapidly. The work is dangerous due to the ever-present risk of explosion and fire.

Roxie's wish of working on the North Slope came true, and so did her wish of building and living in a cabin in the woods, although she admits her home in the woods is accessible by road and not as remote as she originally dreamed.

ROBIN CONNOLLY

I interviewed Robin in her home in Anchorage. We sat at the kitchen table and traded stories about the pioneering days on the North Slope. Robin was guarded at first, but like most of the other interviewees, she eventually found she had a lot to say.

Robin provided intriguing details about walking among wolves and a potentially dangerous encounter with a male wolf.

Robin's account provided details of the Union 798 welders and her respect for them and their work. The pipeline was 798 miles long, the same number as the union. Pipeline union welders were important for the project—and they still travel all over the world to work in dangerous situations. Many have worked together for years with extraordinary camaraderie.

—Carla Williams

Driving School Blues

"My first job was in August of '75. I got this job as a welding rig driver in Prudhoe Bay. The first day I arrived, I was traveling up with a friend from Fairbanks. I remember sitting on the plane and wondering what it was going to be like. She was sitting next to me and she was a laborer and I was a Teamster, and we were both going up there to work.

Previously, I had seen all these people going to work on the pipeline and decided I wanted to go. I thought the best way was through the Culinary Workers Union. I quit my regular job and got a job as a waitress, just long enough to apply for the union. But, when I went down to the hall, I realized I would never get a 'callout'—just too many people.

I was getting frustrated and had quit my regular job, so I went to the job service. I went to this guy and asked him, 'What am I going to do?' I wanted to work and wanted to get on. I told him I'd worked a month at a crummy job and was still nowhere, and wasn't going to get out in the Culinary Union. I said, 'So you've got to tell me something.'

He said, 'Well, don't tell anybody I told you, but there is this Teamster truck driving training and here is the guy who is running it. I cannot promise he will take you—it's mostly to get Natives out on the pipeline, but he does take some women as minorities.'

I thought, 'Well, I've just got to try.' At that time, I wasn't a real assertive person.

Truck driving training wasn't anything super appealing to me, but I decided I just had to do something. I went in and met this man and sat down and said, 'You know, I don't make much money, and I'm the type of person who will save money and not waste it. I really want to get up there and is there anything you can do for me?'

It was so amazing because this guy just looked at me and he said, 'You know, I know you are telling me the truth, and I'd like to help somebody like you get up there.' Most of the people who worked up there did not manage their money, and I saved every paycheck. So, he took me into this truck driving training, which was a month-long course. We drove dump trucks and learned how to drive belly dumps if we wanted to.

I didn't really like it. But, then, I found out they didn't expect all of us to love driving dump trucks. We could also drive school buses as crew drivers. I opted for that. I wanted to get a bus driving job. I didn't want to spend twelve hours a day in a dump truck. I never realized how much it shook you up. It must be bad for your body.

So, that is how I got my dispatch. At the end of the training, I got my dispatch and went to Prudhoe Bay.

I bought the big parka and the insulated pants. I remember taking a world radio with me. The worst thing in my mind was that I didn't have a stereo system I could bring, so I brought this world radio. I got some guy to make an aerial for me, and I could listen all over the world.

Reality Sets In

I remember walking into the mess hall that first night. I didn't have any idea what it was like to walk into a room of about two hundred guys and have them all stop eating and look at me. Nobody told me. I was walking in the cafeteria thinking, 'Uh oh, this is really different! I don't think I'm going to like this!'

I didn't like the thought of driving a school bus full of guys who weren't going to be too excited about having me driving for them. A lot of them never had women working with them before, and they really didn't like putting their lives in a woman's care, so I was nervous. I had no idea what I was doing. I was hoping I wouldn't mess up.

The next day I got to meet this lovely welding rig crew and realized I was the welding rig driver, but it was a pickup truck. They had this crew cab for the two laborers. Laborers could not drive even a pickup. A Teamster had to drive them everywhere.

The laborers' job all day long was to take pieces of plywood and put them on the tundra, so when the welders went to weld, they wouldn't get their cowboy boots dirty. It was their whole job. Maybe they would pick something up at the welder Connex. It was the Teamsters' job to drive the pickup, so the laborers would have someplace to sit because they didn't want the laborers sitting in the welding rigs.

"798-ers" Working on 798 Miles of Pipeline

The welders had a very good skill that was marketable all over the world, and most of them had been in many different countries and many different parts of the United States and were used to travel and working away from home. It was hard work.

I think they had an attitude of superiority, and I suppose if you compare welders to most other construction unions, it is different. If you are in Saudi Arabia working as a welder, you are getting the experience of a culture most unions working in this country don't get.

In a way, I admired their camaraderie. They always wore those little hats [*worn to keep sparks off their heads*]. Most of the time their hats were made by their girlfriends. There was a lot about them to admire or appreciate. They made good money. They had a good skill and they were proud of it.

They were very friendly to women, but I think they had a difficult time believing women were up there to make money for themselves. I believe they had never experienced women under these circumstances, so I think they supposed that women were up there to find boyfriends or husbands. I think part of that was cultural. I think the women they were married to and the women in their families and their neighbors were not all that interested in working up there.

They would always say things like 'sugar' and 'honey' and make all kinds of funny jokes about the idea we were up there to have fun. Of course, they had no idea that, for the average woman working on the Slope, they were not our type at all. They were the last ones we would have been interested in, so there was a kind of cultural shock for them and for us. I'm sure they were used to being 'big

cheeses' everywhere they worked and went in Oklahoma
and Texas, really high on the totem pole.

They make a lot of money—they probably all have
farms or ranches. The pipeline couldn't be built without them and, of course, the pipeline was seven hundred
ninety-eight miles long; the same number as their union.
I think if I had been a little bit older, I might have appreciated them more.

A lot of people just up and quit because they didn't like
the foreman or the crew they were working with. A lot
of the Natives would work just long enough to get some
money. In the Alaska Native culture, you make enough
for what you need. They would come back to work when
the money was gone.

If you were in a good job, you didn't want to quit.
Sometimes it was worth your while to be off and get a
better [*union*] number because the good jobs went to the
people who had been off the longest.

Crew Driver for Bulldozer Men

I got a job centered in Dietrich. I was the driver for a crew
of bulldozer men and bulldozer drivers. There was me as
the driver and a laborer, of course. In the back seat, there
were three guys. So, that was my job, just driving these
three guys.

They really didn't need me. Bulldozer men live on the
bulldozer; they never get off and don't even get down to
take a little walk. They've got their food and their ther-
mos. They are on that dozer for twelve to sixteen hours,
and they are not talking to anybody. They are very interesting people.

All I had to do was take them there and pick them up,
so during the day I was sort of an expediter, which was

great. The foreman would just come up to me and say, 'Would you take this part to that camp?' I got to drive the entire line. I ended up going as far north as Franklin Bluffs and all the way down to the camp just before Fairbanks. That was a wonderful job.

The haul road was very well maintained. Even in the winter, it was never dangerous; everything was perfectly plowed. The only thing that was bad was the dust. If the water trucks didn't get there fast enough, there would be a lot of dust from those huge dump trucks.

Don't Feed the Birds

I always threw my chicken bones out the door for the birds. There were always all these birds around, so, whatever I didn't eat for lunch, I would throw out. One day I was kind of tired and threw the chicken bones out and they didn't go very far, and they dropped next to the crew cab.

There were all these guys working, and all of a sudden, I heard this crunch, crunch, crunch. I thought, 'What is that noise?' and I looked up and there was a brown or grizzly bear eating my chicken bones. The worst part was the danger it presented to all these guys.

The bear must have sneaked up. The next thing there was screaming and jumping and trying to get in crew cabs. Of course, they came to me yelling because I was feeding the bears. I remember feeling very bad, but I was glad nobody got hurt. There was some machinery around and they were all trying to get in it. I promised I would never throw out food again.

The toughest part of that job was talking to the foremen and all the superintendents because they always had time to chat, and when they saw you were a female, they always had time for coffee breaks. I spent a lot of time making small talk with all these foremen and superinten-dents, who were usually from the South.

My parents were coming to visit, so I had to take my R&R, and I left for two weeks. When I went back, my pickup job was gone. They informed me I would then have to drive for a different crew, a backfill crew. It started in Dietrich, but it would be Dietrich, Chandalar, Atigun . . . it just depended on where the pipe was being laid at that time.

Driving a Bus Causes Anxiety

So, now I had a new wave of anxiety because I had to drive a school bus. I hadn't done it since the truck driving training, and it was going to be full of people. Plus, for me, I am not a morning person, so it was difficult because I had to get up early.

I found I had to get all this food together—coffee, water, extra sandwiches, donuts—and I would fill up the whole section of the bus with food; it was part of my job. I did get paid extra. Bus drivers got paid an extra half hour in the morning and an extra half hour in the evening for clean-ing up and setting up. I was lucky to have the job because it was going to pay more money.

I don't know how I lucked out with the backfill crew. People used to come and ask me if I was going to quit, because they wanted my job. My crew got so many hours. After they laid the pipe, then my crew padded it down and rolled it. It had to be this certain density and they tested it. We could never do the backfill until the pipe was laid. After it was laid, they had to do X-rays to make sure nothing changed in the seam of the pipe, so often we would sit all day waiting for the word to go ahead and do the backfill.

Often that word didn't come until three in the afternoon, and we would work until nine or ten at night. So, I would get paid from six-thirty in the morning until a half hour after we got back to camp. During the whole time I worked with that crew, we never got off at five o'clock or even seven; we always worked late. Maybe they set it up politically. I used to wonder about it; we would sit around all day.

I worked out a little deal with my crew. Everything was just a matter of working things out. It didn't take long for me to figure out I couldn't do any expediting; I had to stay with the crew. When they moved, I moved. It was boring. Of course, they would take these little breaks, or we would be sitting there all day together. Most of the time they did have stuff to do, most of the day or at least half the day. Maybe one of the guys would come in for a break and then another one would and of course they always expected me to talk to them.

I convinced them I was more than willing to be extremely sociable with all of them, if they would let me sleep in the morning. We would get out to the work site at about seven-thirty and once I knew we were there, I would take my parka and go in the back and lay down and sleep for three hours. They would come in and have coffee and nobody ever bothered me; nobody ever said anything. When I got up, I'd be 'Miss Sociable.' I'd talk to anybody and laugh at all the jokes. It was a way to manage.

The crew I was with were from Oklahoma. I found things to like about them. The first day I drove that bus, they were silent—a whole busload—they were so scared of a woman driver. I had to drive across little rivers; they didn't make a bridge, so I just had to drive across them. I would be really careful. Other trucks would have been there before, so I saw where the tread went in and followed. The crew cabs would go through, too.

I thought after the first day they were never going to like me and never going to put up with me, but within a few days, they realized I was a much more conscientious driver than a lot of the guys. I was very safe and didn't do drugs. Then they realized they were really lucky.

So, when I woke up from my nap, I had my whole day set; it was two hours for knitting, two hours for nails, two hours for reading, and then I would talk to them when they came in, and I would eat stuff. I think in the beginning I was the only woman, but then this other woman joined our crew. She was an oiler for a crane. She and I would sit together.

She had to oil the crane a half hour in the morning and a half hour in the afternoon and then a half hour at the end of the day, so she had a lot of free time, too. She would work on quilting and we would yak and yak and yak. It was a lot more fun because I had a cohort, and she was quite a cohort because she had been an exotic dancer. So, she had lots of better lines than I had. She was an interesting woman.

Cleaning around the Bears and Wolves

It was not unusual, when I would get out of the bus I was cleaning, to see bears right there. The bears all came to the camps and got into the garbage. It didn't matter what they built. They built these big wooden things with wooden tops. I remember one time, walking through one of the trailer barracks and seeing this bear flipping open this big wooden thing. Then the wooden thing would crash down on the bear's head, but it would keep taking food. I used to sit, especially in Atigun and Chandalar, and watch the bears go up these mountains in about two minutes.

The other thing I loved were the wolves. They got to know the school buses, so they associated us with food and would wait for us. I never fed them myself. There would be the whole pack, just sitting there waiting, and they would trot along behind the bus. It was so amazing to watch them. The female who had the puppies would come forward and sit and politely beg, and the males would be stationed in strategic positions, and the puppies would be in the bushes. I used to see them every day, but I never fed them. Someone was feeding them, though.

One time, I was taking a walk down the right-of-way and passed a crew and they said, 'Be careful; there are wolves ahead.' I wasn't afraid because I saw them all the time on my little walks. They would just be walking the other way. They are amazing animals; you can just feel how intelligent they are.

I just kept walking and soon I saw a bus and there was the female begging and the male in the strategic position, and I just sort of walked through them. I knew as long as I didn't bother anybody, it was okay.

Then I walked a little farther and heard this whimpering in the bushes, so I just stopped, and the puppies ran across the road. I just waited and was going to continue walking. All of a sudden, I turned and looked and there was a big male sitting there looking at me as if to say, 'As long as you don't do anything, you are fine. But make a move for those puppies and you are dead meat.'

He wasn't threatening or mean-looking. The puppies were right in front of me. I didn't know what to do, so I just stopped. They eventually wandered away. They are very interesting animals.

Clearing a Grand a Week

I didn't have to make my bed; I didn't have to cook; I didn't have to spend time going shopping. All my needs were met, and I was making the most money I had ever

made in my life. I cleared a thousand a week. Sometimes
I got paid for twenty-four hours. At that time, it was fan-
tastic. I didn't have any complaints; I loved the nature.
I would have preferred a different social life. Having so
many men and so few women wasn't as enjoyable as one
would think.

Substandard Women's Dorm

At Chandalar, the women's trailer was just awful—lousy
rooms, lousy bathrooms. By that time, there was another woman on my crew. We decided we didn't want
to stay in the women's dorms; we wanted to stay in the
men's dorms.

We went to the men's dorm and asked them all if it
would bother them if we had a room there. We didn't
mind seeing them in the morning if they didn't mind seeing us in the morning. They said sure. They put little flowers on one of the stalls and left it nice for us.

I was twenty-five and these guys were nineteen to
twenty-three. While we were there, it was lovely. They
would get off work at five or six and they would do their
drinking and by nine o'clock they were out. It was really
a quiet place.

The quarters were clean, with two beds, two closets, two
night tables, and maybe two bureaus, really small. I never
spent a lot of time in my room, so I don't remember much
about it. I was in there for five hours between midnight
and five in the morning.

The evening was so much fun. The earliest we would
get back was nine o'clock, so I would just eat dinner, have
a couple drinks with my crew, and then go and have my
social life. I just loved it. It was truly the historical happening. Everybody was always in a good mood; we were all
making good money.

In one room, you would have a lot of long hairs, and in the room right next to them, the guys would be playing country-western music and drinking whiskey. Women were welcome anywhere. All you had to do was say, 'Hi, I like this music, can I come in?' I didn't do that, but I did get to know a lot of people.

There was always this socializing. The only work you did was on the job; other than that, it was just having fun. Every day was the same; there was the work part and the fun part. I never stayed up all night or anything, but I was always sort of sleep-deprived.

I remember I brought up my cross-country skis, thinking that people pay to come and look at this stuff. Here was all this gorgeous scenery. The younger people from Alaska appreciated it, but to others it was just this boring place where they had to go to make money. Maybe they didn't think it was beautiful. They certainly didn't act impressed.

I can remember driving back from the job and the crew would always be so tired. I would have tapes of music for the guys from the South and tapes for those who were younger. I have very good memories of playing that music. For example, I would play Pink Floyd for my generation. I can remember driving back to the camp and they would all be relaxed. In many ways, at least I was with a crew I had some feeling for.

Sleeping on the Job

People did have a habit of sleeping a lot. If people didn't have to work very hard, they would just go to sleep. It was never unusual to drive by and see people sleeping. It was part of the job.

When I had the crew cab and I had the laborer, we had to go someplace. We were really close to the other crew, so we went to say hi to them. We drove by their work site and the whole crew was sleeping. There was not one person awake and not one person woke up. It was like in a movie where everybody was dead, or a drug was dropped from the sky.

People were sitting in the crane, in the bus, in their pickup. We just kind of went by and said, 'Well, we just won't wake them up.' The poor laborers—the young ones—wouldn't have enough sense to get some sleep; they would be up all night and they would be up digging ditches and carrying things the next morning."

———————————

Robin's North Slope days are over, but she says she will always remember the interesting people and memories of the exciting time in history, when much of the Alaska population was connected in some way to the same project, the building of the Trans-Alaska Pipeline.

ROSEMARY CARROLL

Rosemary is an energetic, highly qualified control room board operator who worked for many years on the North Slope. She typifies the technical female Slope worker in her knowledge of the petroleum business.

The board operator manages panels of gauges and lights, monitoring pressure, temperature, level, and flow of a facility's vessels, pipelines, tanks, and so on. In real time, the board operator ensures the safety of the overall system and people working in the facilities. While an oil processing facility includes numerous independent high-pressure systems automatically regulated through safety features, it requires human oversight in case something goes wrong or a system is out of service for repairs or other reasons.

Due to a last-minute change in plans, Rosemary was not on the fateful 1987 plane that crashed on a flight from Kenai to Anchorage. Her first days on the North Slope were very different from other new hires because of the crash, but she took it all in stride and adapted to the situation. In this interview, Rosemary described a control system upset, which caused excitement, but also stress.

—Carla Williams

The Crash

"I was working at Trading Bay as a roustabout and came up to the Slope in November, then went back to Trading Bay and was hired just before Christmas on December 23. I was scheduled on a flight at six in the morning from Kenai to Anchorage. The night before, a friend of mine in Anchorage who was going through a divorce called and

wanted me to come and spend time with her. So, I didn't
tell anybody and just jumped a plane.

When I went to the Anchorage airport the following
morning to go to the Slope to start my job, I was sitting
there waiting and heard that the Southcentral [*Air*] plane
from Kenai, the flight I was supposed to be on, had just
crashed! It was 1987. Five people who died on that plane
worked at Kuparuk, two from Central Process Facility 1.

My family thought I was on that plane, which is why it is
so easy for me to remember my first day on the Slope. My
mom and brothers called all over the Slope because they
didn't know exactly where to find me. They had called
Southcentral when they heard the news.

I had met the guys who died when I came up to interview, but I didn't remember them. I had just come off
eighteen weeks in Trading Bay. I got off work and went
straight to the interview, so I didn't believe I did very
good. I babbled something, then came out and said to
myself, 'Well I screwed that one up!' Then I got the call to
come up and interview on the Slope.

After the crash, walking into CPF-1 that first day was
just awful. Here I was the new person up there. It's like
when you work with a crew for so long, the operators are
cloistered. It's your own little world with blinders on, and
you get so close they become like family to you. It was just
devastating for them.

It was real quiet the first week; nobody said anything.
Everyone was crying. I went around from area to area and
worked with this operator and that. Everything stopped.
Some K shift people came up to cover for the J shift people
who went to the funerals, so they came up for the day.

Here they had lost part of their family and [*they must
have wondered,*] 'Who is this new person here? What is she
doing here?' I always felt it, but especially then. It was like
I was a replacement for those guys. It was really awful;

I stayed real quiet. I listened to them if they wanted to talk. I didn't ask a whole lot of questions that first week. I did a lot of reading on my own. Mainly, they were nice.

If you stand back and watch things and listen, you stand a whole lot better chance of figuring out what is going on. It's when you dive and barge into something, like a lot of people do, that's not good.

For some new people, it was like, 'I'm here and I'm going to change this place and I have all the experience you have.' It's hard to overcome a first impression.

Proving Yourself

We had Mary, Rose, Molly, Donna, and Jill. There was a pile of women at CPF-1, so if you were a real antagonistic kind of guy, you could have said, 'We've got enough already.'

In the field itself, there were no 'shrinking violets.' Honestly. None. If they showed up, they didn't last very long, especially in those days. You couldn't be thin-skinned. You had to not only be able to take it, [*but*] you [*also*] had to be able to toss it back, if you know what I mean. You had to earn the respect of your coworkers, or you were going to be very temporary.

Being a woman on the Slope, you always have to prove yourself. It's a daily thing. They are waiting for you to screw up. You stick out more; people watch you more. You are more in the spotlight.

I go to bed at eight-thirty at night. I get into this routine. I eat certain things for breakfast. For example, I have two muffins and coffee for breakfast and I eat them over at the plant. I walk down the hallway and walk outside to go over to the plant. I look up at the stacks to see if they are going or if the flare is burning normally instead of lit up like a firecracker. If those things are okay, the day holds promise, and I can eat my muffins.

Everyone who has trained on the [*control*] board sits there all day, rolling their chair from screen to screen. They don't want to get up; that's a little too much trouble, so they roll from screen to screen.

But, at the end of the day, I've never been so exhausted. I drag myself back to my room and crawl on my bed and just pass out, and I wake up at three o'clock in the morning, still dressed. That's how exhausted I am, because I am waiting and thinking about what's going to happen. Alarm! Oh! And I jump! I am thinking I don't have a clue what I will do if the shit hits the fan, but I really do.

Screaming Gas Leak

There was this engineer who came from town and walked into the control room and said, 'There is nothing going on; this is a tedious little job.' He was pretty much full of his own importance and stuff.

It was funny because the next day we had a huge leak outside next to the primary at the injection line. A guy came in and said, 'Hey, I think you have a hole in your primary.' The oil operator went out and said, 'Bill you'd better come down here.' So, Bill went down there, and I was on the board waiting.

Nobody was calling, so I finally said, 'Hey, could somebody tell me what's going on?' Bill said, 'Hey, we got a major problem out here.' I could hear the screaming of the gas leak behind him. I said, 'Is it the primary?' My hands were on the shutdown button, and Bill said, 'No, it's the four thousand psi [*pounds per square inch*] gas-injection line.'

We had to shut down all our gas-injection recip [*reciprocating*] compressors to drop the pressure on the line, which handled all our injection gas. It was about 120 million scfd [*standard cubic feet per day*]. So, here was this humongous flare and we had tons of alarms going off. And here came this engineer, prancing in with his eyes popping out and his lip quivering, with the noise and the controlled chaos. People were running around and saying, 'Get him out of here!'

On the board, you don't want to shut things in. With your fans and coolers, you've got to be aware of the temperature with those—shutting those down. Your anti-ice on the turbines stops the icing conditions. There are plenty of things you are going to want to watch when it gets cold, but the equipment is usually happy when it's cold. It's strong. In the summer months, when the air is denser, the turbines don't run efficiently. That's when you close all your big gas wells because the turbines get bogged down and can't handle it.

Frostbitten Fingers

I despise the cold. I used to feel I had to be out there hammering up flanges outside in sixty below. I'd have to be right there, because if they were suffering, I'd have to suffer. I'm way past that.

The sandjet driver's out there and he works in the cold a lot. I come out and I don't like the cold, so I've got these coveralls on, and I've got the bunny boots on, and I've got the face mask on, and I've got the down vest and the parka. And I'm trying to get up on the vessel and he is laughing, because it's not that cold to him. I've worked outside too many times. I've worked outside all my life. My fingers have been frostbitten. I've fished and I've 'deck-handed' and I've been cold for twenty years outside.

I miss my son the most. I've missed half his life. When I'm on vacation, it screws up his schedule. Because he is a boy of routine, he says, 'Aren't you supposed to be going back to work? Not that I want you to.' It's all he has ever known.

I'm blessed that the people I work with are great; it makes all the difference. You can deal with almost anything if you have a little humor in it and if you have the right people beside you. I am lucky enough to have taken a different path than most . . . to have worked with some of the finest people, whom I call my friends, and have the adventure of working in a field that is challenging, changing constantly, and tests you when you least expect it. It's been a good life, and I have very few regrets. What a time it was and what a ride it's been."

Rosemary commuted from Soldotna to Kuparuk Oil Field for years. She retired as a board operator at a Kuparuk CPF but finds herself returning to the North Slope from time-to-time after retirement in Arizona. She loves working as an operator and considers her colleagues her lifelong friends.

CLARA KING

Clara's flamboyant style echoes a past life when she was a professional stand-up comedian. Her humor appears in her everyday speech, along with an unmistakable Southern drawl. Clara described how bullcooks didn't cook and how she put Coke cans under her bed to keep them cold. She was ready to leave when she first arrived at sixty-five below zero, but she stayed and ended up working for eleven years on the North Slope.

—*Carla Williams*

Bullcooks

"I came up on a culinary call. I went up the first part of 1974 and worked off and on until 1991. I started out on the D list and worked my way up. I was dispatched from the union hall as a bullcook.

When I got to the union hall, I was way overdressed when I applied for this job. I had on a knit suit, gold jewelry, and a fur hat. Everybody else had on jeans and a T-shirt, so I immediately got rid of my good clothes and went over to Sears, or whatever was in Fairbanks at the time, and bought jeans and T-shirts.

I said jokingly to the BA [*business agent*] that I wanted a job on the pipeline and didn't care if I had to clean toilets or make beds. And he said, 'That's what a bullcook does.' I said, 'You're shittin' me!' He said, 'No, I'm not.' I said, 'I thought that meant somebody who works in the kitchen.' He said, 'No, they're called kitchen helpers.'

A bullcook is an old logging term. It goes back to the old logging days when the men would go out to cut the logs. They would leave someone behind to take care of the camp and the oxen; he was called the bullcook. That term just kind of stuck. On the Slope, a bullcook means someone who cleans the barracks and makes the bed.

Kitchen Helper

So, when I got up to Franklin Bluffs, the camp was not quite completed. The construction workers were there building the camps, but there were no 'pipeliners' at that time. So, they put me in the kitchen as a kitchen worker. [*It wasn't until later that Clara worked as a bullcook.*] I followed this black lady around. I later adopted her as my black momma. She kind of showed me the ropes about working in the kitchen. I didn't know how to work in the kitchen; all I knew is what I did at home.

For example, we had to cut the pies or desserts and put them out to be served, because we served four meals a day. I worked the day shift, so we prepared the lunch and dinner. She told me to slice the pie, so I just started slicing the pie like you would normally do at home. She said, 'No, no, no; there's a way to slice a pie.' Just little things like that . . . only the kitchen people know.

Then I found out about a bullcook's job at the women's barracks. There were over 350 men in camp and 28 women. If you brought your own bedspread, then you had to make your own bed. If you used camp facility blankets and sheets, then the housekeeper or bullcook would go in and clean.

We were not allowed to move anything on the desk— and you know the women always had a bunch of clutter on their desk. So, all I basically had to do was empty their garbage and vacuum once a week.

I would make anywhere from two to four beds a day. I had a real clean hallway and bathroom, because that was back in the days when we would get twelve hours a day to do one barrack, which later changed. But I didn't stay as a housekeeper very long, because the goal was to get out as a Teamster.

Teamster

I started out working in the warehouse in Franklin Bluffs as a Teamster. I did inventory on parts, like Caterpillar. We worked in the 'cat house.' I called home and told my dad what I was doing and he said, 'Oh, my God, have the Teamsters organized that, too?' I did that until I got my four hundred hours to get my A card, which didn't take too long because I was getting long hours.

Then I became an expediter. We went up and down the pipeline back in those days. From Franklin Bluffs, I worked my way down to Happy Valley, then Galbraith Lake, then Dietrich, then Atigun. Everything was south of Franklin Bluffs; the only thing north was Prudhoe Bay. Atigun was a small camp and very quiet. There were probably no more than four hundred people at the most. I was in camps that went up to twenty-two hundred, so this was like a little tiny camp. Everybody had fun. Everybody had special attention, just because it was so small. After work, we'd sit around and drink and tell stories and watch movies.

Little Privacy

On the actual pipeline, some of the camps were the pits. Some of them were really old trailers. Some of the trailers were kind of square and they had eight rooms and they were tiny. If anyone was doing anything in the other room, you knew about it, much worse than the ATCO trailers, which came later. Prime Camp at Prudhoe Bay was luxury compared to these rooms; they were horrible.

When we first went up there, it was really hard to get a telephone, and people would stand [*in line*] for hours and bang on the door if you took too long. Eventually, they got more telephone lines. People liked to call home once a week or more. They were making all that money with nowhere to spend it; at least they wanted to call home. On the North Slope, the telephone lines were few and far between, so they didn't get to make that many phone calls, and that was inconvenient.

When I first went up there, my daughter was about nine. She stayed in Texas and lived with her dad and my mom, and when she was in ninth grade, she went to a boarding school.

Entertainment

Up there, money was just no object after a while, because on the line what you saw was your check, which was just a piece of paper. You really didn't have anywhere to spend money until R&R. Back in those days, we would work anywhere from nine to twenty-two weeks. It was like the outside world didn't exist, because, at that time, if you did get news, it was videotaped and flown up.

We didn't have cable. When I first went up there, we didn't even have television and very little radio, so we just entertained ourselves. We usually got newspapers every two or three days. Eventually, we did have television. They actually videotaped shows from Anchorage or Fairbanks and they would fly the tapes up there. Some of those guys had short wave.

We would try to get together and socialize. There was always something—somebody's birthday, somebody getting married, somebody getting divorced. You would take a shower and get dressed and you'd be ready to party.

One of my favorite jobs was as entertainment director at Prudhoe Bay. I put together a small theater and booked a lot of 1950s bands like the Coasters, Drifters, and Platters. The Platters said they had been all over the world and this was the most interesting place they had been. We had a lot of dances and marathons. My job was taking care of the people after their long and busy workdays. We didn't charge anything; we just had fun."

———————————

Clara retired from Nordstrom in Anchorage, where she worked after leaving the Slope. She remembers her days on the Slope fondly and recalls the many friends she made and the fun she had organizing the festivities. Clara appeared on a Discovery Channel television special about the pipeline, which played for five years across the country. On both the pipeline's thirtieth and fortieth anniversary, NBC-KTUU interviewed Clara about her experiences working on the pipeline. She can often be found in Anchorage volunteering as an entertainer or host for a charity event.

SAMANTHA GEORGE

Journeyman electrician Samantha (Sam) George is a contemporary young woman working in a predominately male profession. This interview, which occurred in 2015, gives a recent perspective of a female Slope worker.

Samantha is a five-foot-two, petite woman who doesn't have trouble carrying the heavy load of bulky clothes and tools around all day. She describes herself as "stocky with muscle." Sam, as she likes to be called, experienced no discrimination and recalled only positive experiences in this first year on the North Slope.

—Carla Williams

"I did my apprenticeship with the International Brotherhood of Electrical Workers (IBEW) apprenticeship school. I just wanted a good-paying job. I took a couple of college classes when I got out of high school, but I didn't apply myself. I didn't know what I wanted to do. I needed some direction.

My dad is a non-union electrician, so he suggested I try to get into the IBEW apprenticeship, because he felt it was the best one with good benefits and good education. I did an initial interview, but I needed to do something to prove my skills so they would hire me. So, I went to Job Corps out in Palmer for an electrical pre-apprenticeship program.

That helped me get into the IBEW the next time I interviewed. The apprenticeship was about four and one-half years, which was a long time to devote. It was a good experience for different types of work.

For the most part, people are very accepting. I think sometimes there are different expectations. I just always do the best I can to meet or exceed expectations. I have had a very positive experience on the Slope. Being union, I am used to making the same wage as everybody else. For what I have seen, my wage is comparable to others at the same skill level.

I don't think about being a woman until I see another woman around and it surprises me. Most people treat me just like any of the other workers. I think sometimes people can be uncomfortable because they are worried they will say the wrong thing. I think people might be paranoid about harassment lawsuits. When people get to know me a little bit, they just talk to me like the other guys.

Occasionally, there is a little bit of unwanted attention. I solve that problem on my own. It is very easy to say, 'Hey, I'm married.' That usually ends it right there. During my apprenticeship, I was used to being around more females in the IBEW. The IBEW and the other union trades are proactive in trying to recruit female workers, so I was around other females a lot more. It seems like there wasn't that kind of attention then.

There are a lot more women in the summertime and they tend to be college age. The ones year-round are a mixture of girls in their twenties to mid-fifties. I met a woman electrician in passing at lunch in the chow hall. We just talked about how different it was to see another female electrician.

I get to Anchorage a day ahead, so I do not miss the plane. My sister lives in Anchorage, so I stay with her and her family; that works out nice and keeps me from missing the flight. Missing your flight to the Slope is an automatic reprimand.

When I started out, I worked a lot in the main facilities installing cables, panels, and heat trace. I am now working in the field. My tool partner and I each have a truck in case we need to convoy in inclement weather during phase conditions. We travel to the different drill sites and the wells and disconnect instruments and power to the wells prior to the rig's arrival. After the rig is done, we hook it back up.

Sometimes I work on the 'highline' crew with high-voltage cables for power to the rigs. The safety culture is very strict to prevent incidents. If we did happen to be around a cable where there is the potential of being energized or having residual energy, we have personal protective equipment for that. Generally, when we don that equipment, it has been mostly to test a circuit to verify it is de-energized.

There is a point when they shut down all the work outside. To work outside during shutdown, you need paperwork signed by the higher-ups saying it was okay. You need frequent warm-up breaks. I have insulated gloves. Everything takes a lot longer and it is labor-intensive because you have on heavy Arctic gear so you don't get cold. It is heavy and wears you out. I don't usually have too hard of time, but I can tell the difference after a long day.

I miss home-cooked food. They do a good job with food, but sometimes I just have a craving for something. If I am home, I can just cook it, but up there you don't have that kind of choice. I miss my husband, obviously. Working on the Slope is not for everyone, but I feel grateful I have my job.

One of the toughest things is I tend to be a peacemaker. I like it when everyone gets along. For some reason, being up there intensifies people's idiosyncrasies; sometimes there is tension. I like it when everything goes smooth. There is a term for the tension; it's called 'Slope opera.'

Everyone tries to help each other out. I don't feel singled out at all. People can cuss and swear, but I cuss and swear, too. One of my mentors is my instructor from Job Corps, and I still keep in touch with him. He is a wealth of knowledge about the Slope. It seems like anytime I talk to him, he knows something about it.

Pete is also one of my mentors and a colleague and a fellow union member. One of my tool partners, Travis, has been up there for a long time and he knows all the tricks if we need something. He knows who to talk to if we need a tool you can't get anywhere else. He circumvents difficulties that may arise and that is pretty cool.

Being an electrician is a really great trade for women to get into and they should not be discouraged by this preconceived notion it is a man's job, because it is not. It is everyone's job who works for it. At the apprenticeship school, there were a lot of married women with children, but it's rare on the Slope. It's good for family life. It's a good job all around."

––––––––––

Samantha lives in California with her husband and commutes to the Slope on a three-week-on, three-week-off work schedule. They spend their time sharing the repairs and making improvements on a new home. They also like to visit breweries, hike, and cook healthy meals. Samantha's husband takes care of chores that arise when she is working on the Slope, unless it is electrical—then it waits for Sam.

PART THREE

NORTH
TO THE
FUTURE

*The question isn't who's going to let
me; it's who's going to stop me.*

—Ayn Rand

THE FLOW CONTINUES

When the first workers ventured to Alaska to work on the Trans-Alaska Pipeline Project, everyone came for the project duration, except the project never really ended. Workers were pleasantly surprised to find that the gift kept on giving. During the up times, union workers made overtime pay over forty hours, double-time pay on Sundays, and triple-time pay on holidays. The down times were rough, such as in the eighties, when bumper stickers read: 'Dear Lord, give me another boom and I promise I won't screw it up this time.' But, for the most part, the oil flowed nonstop and construction continued.

Every day, planes fly hundreds of workers to the North Slope for work. New oil deposits keep the drills buzzing, and, periodically, camps are packed with workers. Oil prices drop, and people wonder if the end is near, but then prices rise, and workers return.

Thousands of acres of potential oil reserves on the North Slope, some off-limits to oil companies, lure politicians to periodically examine drilling the resources. Sometimes the investors succeed, and off-limit areas are opened. The Arctic National Wildlife Refuge (ANWR) and National Petroleum Reserve in Alaska (NPRA) are two such areas. In 2016, ConocoPhillips started the first oil development in the NPRA since its creation in 1923. Inevitably, additional areas to drilling will open.

Pressures to drill often overshadow environmental issues, such as the controversial subsea drilling in the Chukchi and Beaufort Seas. These are frontiers in the quest for future oil. The Alaska oil-field project could last for years, offering the excitement of living and working in the remote wilderness possible for many.

The eager twenty-year-old men and women who cannot wait for their first North Slope paycheck compete for positions held by old-timers who have worked there for years. The experienced veterans are slow to retire because the companies need their expertise. Some have been there since the beginning and know the facilities inside and out.

Commuting is routine for them as they fly to and from the Lower 48 and exotic places like Indonesia and Costa Rica. The "two and two" or "three and three" work schedules provide an exciting life for those interested in adventures around the world. Some won't quit until they are paid off with large severance packages. Others will expire there. The majority will leave their legacy and move on.

No matter what generation occupies a camp bed, working outside in the extreme cold challenges the most robust person. Workers still warm up in constantly running vehicles or warm-up shacks, just as in the past. The camps have improved, but rooms are still cramped, and construction camp rooms are worn.

Improved accommodations, though, do not diminish the initial shock of landing at the Deadhorse airport on a still and cold January. Arriving from Florida or Arizona equates to a ninety-degree difference. A fifty-below-zero wind chill is not uncommon. At that temperature, the portable tarmac staircase is often slippery and the cold handrail stings through gloves. Empty buses sit motionless like Buckingham Palace sentries, waiting to accept passengers for the frozen journey to camps.

Driving on the North Slope feels, in many areas, like one continuous construction zone. In the winter, snow packs thicken on road signs like cement, making them useless. Periodic checkpoint security guards or machines review badges for validity; otherwise, the miles and miles of roads to wells or production facilities are seemingly endless and monotonous. The white snow confuses newcomers who easily lose direction. Snow-packed winter roads turn into muddy mush in spring and dusty whirlwinds in summer.

Large truck wheels throw rocks from the road, so safety rules forbid walking or jogging. A plume of dust and dirt may follow a large truck, obscuring a passing vehicle, so many follow behind in dusty or snowy conditions. Modules or drilling rigs several stories high travel the same roads as the cars and trucks and may impede traffic for hours.

Broadcasting traffic tickets throughout the companies encourages drivers to behave. Accidents require teams performing an event analysis in which results sometimes end in permanent termination. Safety is taken seriously.

North Slope companies maintain zero tolerance for alcohol and drugs. During pipeline construction and in the early startup years, alcohol and drugs prevailed. Innovative transportation methods into the camps included driving liquor past guard shacks in loader buckets and hiding drugs in construction materials. Back then, airport luggage checks and X-ray machines were nonexistent.

Traffic around the processing facilities increases during construction, but when away from them, constant winds blowing across the tundra is the only sound. Insect noise permeates in summer. Just like the television documentaries with helicopter cameras panning Alaska's rugged mountaintops, silver valleys, and braided rivers shimmering in the sun, the North Slope environment enchants workers and visitors. The stunning scenery excites even the hard-core curmudgeon.

I remember a friend enticing me to take a walk across the tundra before restrictions protected the environment. As we walked, I realized the small earthen bumps (pingos) in the distance appeared quite high. After an hour, he said to watch for polar bears because they liked to hide behind the pingos. I immediately walked back to the camp and never walked on tundra again.

Everyone wanted a truck to drive to the ocean, but they were a luxury usually saved for management, so the lucky people drove their coworker friends on road trips to the Arctic Ocean. I drove there several times and walked along the beach. I saw discarded whalebones and a few pieces of driftwood, but otherwise the beach appeared barren. Evenly matched, half-inch- to inch-sized rocks defined the shore. Polar bears roam the beach, so danger lurks everywhere along the Arctic Ocean.

Besides sightseeing, dining tops the list of activities on the North Slope. Cafeterias provide low-calorie food, such as salads and vegetables, and everything is free and abundant. Meals no longer include all-you-can-eat king crab, filet mignon, and lobster, but workers line up on prime rib and steak nights. Weeks drag on, and, for some workers, food provides comfort and consolation for working in the harsh conditions.

Typical long work schedules, such as the twelve-week-on, two-week-off schedule I worked in the eighties, no longer exist. Some people worked months on end without breaks. Today, most workers show for two or three weeks and then leave for a week or two. For safety reasons, some companies now require advance approval for working longer than regular work days or weeks.

The long workdays can nurture long-lasting friendships with coworkers and even partnerships. Some people started relationships and others divorced. Maintaining a marriage with the off-and-on schedule challenges even the strongest relationships. Some women reluctantly found themselves in relationships and others went there to find partners. It all seemed so ordinary at the time. Making friends, nurturing relationships, working day after day, sleeping, eating, and partying. Few admit to doing something as spectacular as blazing a trail, but they did more than blaze a trail—they made profound history.

Gender is probably the most restricting force in American life.

—Gloria Steinem[11]

AFTERWORD

Why did these trailblazers seek work in the isolated North Slope environment, forgoing basic psychological needs and comforts? Surely the money drew them in, but also power and adventure, or simply an attraction to something different, something beyond their mothers' imagination. Some women mention the thrill of being the first or among a group of firsts. Certainly, for most, it is difficult to pinpoint a motivation while swept up in a "movement" of an era, a movement of changing times and environments.

Most people making a profound difference in society and even those bestowed awards feel uncomfortable acknowledging achievements, because people don't experience life in a vacuum; their experiences are filled with friends, family, and coworkers who provide a shared experience. None of the women in this book will admit to a trailblazing title, but they embodied the definition of trailblazers as a group and as individuals. Celebrating their achievement is a consistent theme in this book.

There are, of course, many other women pathbreakers whose stories should and, hopefully, will be told someday. There are, no doubt, countless incidents in which these and other women provide a role model for many females wanting to forge ahead in a man's world. It is no longer a strange sight in Alaska or anywhere in the United States to see a woman operating a front-end loader or a woman's face as the welding hood lifts.

The book's dialogue between past and present focuses on change and, in some cases, the lack of change. These collected stories reflect a long stretch of pipeline history and highlight gender equality as a contemporary concern with historical roots. As the issues of gender equality, respect, and equal pay evolve, we need to remember, as the Athabascan Alaska author Velma Wallis suggests in her book, *Raising Ourselves,* that the past needs to be understood to help illuminate the path forward. She asks: "How can you write about the storm if you are still in it?"[12]

Now, years later, we can try to understand an era and celebrate accomplishments. The overarching lessons addressed in this book, which helped the individual women advance within their professional lives, center on respect and equal pay for equal work. Their struggle for personal and professional recognition occurred during a unique time when a generation of men and women began challenging and breaking barriers on many levels.

Over the centuries, women and indigenous people have not held the public's attention as much as white male recollections, but that is changing as women of all colors and indigenous people write their own narratives, like these interviews. Certainly, female voices and perspectives provide balance against the analysis of historic pipeline events written by men.

During the pipeline construction, the proposed Equal Rights Amendment changed the social and political landscape in the Lower 48; however, the road was rough. High-achieving women and gender biases still lingered in everyday situations. In her notations about women on the pipeline in "Femininity on Alaska's North Slope," Julia Feuer-Cotter, characterizes Alaska during this time as a new frontier and the women as modern-day pioneers pushing boundaries.

Since then, in some areas, the change is slow. Nitin Nohria, the Dean of Harvard Business School, said in a recent interview:

"We have to all collectively realize that there have been many, many years in which the talents and achievements of women, not for any deliberate reasons, but for subtle reasons, tend to be underestimated, just by a little bit. In a competitive world, all it takes is to be underestimated by a little bit for discrimination to take root."[13]

A 2013 study comparing the percentages of women and men in leadership positions in the American oil industry concluded: "Still no progress after years of no progress."[14]

Within the oil industry, however, some changes have been made, although still not the significant changes we dreamed of in the seventies. Today, in Alaska's oil field, women managers celebrate to themselves if more than one or two women sit in a conference room filled with men. The lack of women is evident in corporate photos of boards of directors and other business images.

The resource-extracting industry remains a male-dominated one, although female engineers, project engineers and managers are making inroads. Women who work in the Alaska oil industry today still encounter barriers, particularly in management-level pay. Even though there are many more women in oil and gas, and some have achieved senior levels, the "good ol' boy" environment remains.

This gender-biased environment continues to hinder equal opportunities for women in the industry. In a 2014 NES Global Talent study of 272 women engineers [*Women-in-engineering-report-single_final-1.pdf*], respondents said that "they did not receive the same recognition for their work as male peers, feeling as if they must work harder to prove themselves." One respondent commented that women are sometimes viewed as having been hired only because the company wanted to create the image of diversity.[15]

Yet progress occurs, which attests to the relentless work of many female oil pioneers. Although women leaders emerged in some top positions at the large oil companies, there appears to be less change for oil-field service contractors, in general, and middle management, in particular.

Women oil-field board operators and drill site operators on the North Slope are not mentored as much as in the past, according to the women interviewed in this book, maybe because of more competition for fewer positions. Sam George mentioned the numerous women attending the IBEW apprenticeship program, but also said few women electricians made it to Slope positions. In fact, she only met one other woman electrician at Kuparuk.

The lack of women on the North Slope may be due to working in a barren and isolated environment. The interviews certainly allude to these issues. Irene Bartee, for instance, waited for someone to provide leadership but found she was alone in making decisions, so she forged ahead—although she mentioned that if she had had anyone to quit to, she would have quit. She provided leadership in an uncertain vacuum, which must have felt empowering, but also lonely and isolating.

Onice McClain describes missing a family life, an opportunity that is lost forever. Donna Ford raises issues around the lack of privacy and the oppressive Rule J, which stated that males could not talk to females, except about business during business hours. Dana Martinez Parker acknowledged very few places that felt private, not even the sanctuary of her room.

A woman at the top will often face a lonely position, simply due to a lack of reliable mentors. The much younger Samantha George seems at ease, but her tenure is short.

Many women workers and their female peers remained in the industry after the initial pipeline construction concluded. Today, the first generation of pipeline workers are in their sixties, seventies, and eighties and rapidly retiring. Thanks to the pathbreaking work of these pioneer wildcat women and an affirmative action plan that secured a diverse workforce, there is progress in overall gender equality and pay but very little long-term change in the absolute numbers of women in the oil industry.

Yes, women want equal pay for equal work, but they also want respect. Women workers on the North Slope demanded respect and achieved it, which is evident in these interviews. We should all take to heart the words of Gloria Steinem, who once said: "Once we give up searching for approval, we often find it easier to earn respect."

FEMININITY ON ALASKA'S NORTH SLOPE

by Julia Feuer-Cotter
Arctic Environmental Historian

When the Trans-Alaska Pipeline System (TAPS) was proposed in 1969, the common rules in the construction camps were "no booze, no drugs, and no women."[16] As in other projects, the first two rules were commonly violated, but the third prohibition had to be entirely suspended due to an issue larger than proclivities: namely, large-scale social changes. This change was foremost driven by the fight for gender equality in the workplace.

Consequently, the Trans-Alaska Pipeline Authorization Act of 1973 mandated an affirmative action plan that required women be hired and contribute to the pipeline project. This requirement nullified that third common rule, which was, until then, deeply knitted into the fabric of the construction trade. This change to the structure of the trade—namely, the contribution of women beyond traditional female work roles—was met with initial resistance and anxiety.

This book addresses how the women made use of the wider social change to break into the male-dominated workplace of the pipeline construction. The collected interviews illustrate how Alaska, as the setting for this project and imagined as a frontier, empowered women not only to assume traditionally masculine work roles, but also to penetrate the male-constructed geographical space.

Many frontiers have excited and challenged Americans over multiple generations, and Alaska is often still referred to as "the Last Frontier." Alaska's history is filled with the imagery and symbolism of the frontier, and the concept of Alaska as the Last Frontier is deeply manifested in the self-reflection of most Alaskans.[17] To describe this concept more clearly, cultural critics use terminology like *frontier romance*[18] and *post-western landscape*[19] to refer to these associations.

While both concepts extend to women in the landscape, the setting of the frontier is primarily understood as a masculine space.[20] Some historians argue that it is here that the modern "American Adam," a cultural symbol of the (exclusively white) new man in a new territory, explores the outskirts of civilization and adds economic development to the landscape.

The story of the American Adam is based on white male Europeans who had been corrupted by an industrialized civilization and who were reborn upon arrival in the New World. The settler became a new man—the American Adam, as R. W. B. Lewis named him in his influential 1950s study with the same title.[21]

In this book, Lewis analyzed nineteenth-century literature and concluded it was the myth of the West rather than the actual physical space that enabled the unique American self-reflection as new man. The image of the American Adam is closely linked to the understanding of the frontier landscape as receptive and where nature can be dominated by physical strength.

These characteristics of the geographical space were seen to offer an opportunity to exhibit masculine traits and pursue male trades, which include dominating nature. The understanding of Alaska as imagined frontier space meant that the people who would push this frontier would traditionally identify with a version of the American Adam and foster a space that excluded women.

At the peak of construction activity on the pipeline, in October 1975, the TAPS service and construction company Alyeska employed more than seventy thousand laborers, engineers, administrators, drivers, drillers, and other skilled and unskilled workers.[22] Women's positions made up 7 percent of the jobs within this diverse workforce.[23] These women challenged traditional gender identity in the workplace by laboring in typically male-dominated trades such as welding, surveying, construction, and truck driving.

Not only was the work demanding, but it also took place in an extremely challenging environment. As the stories collected in this book illustrate, the shared experience of being in the Alaska landscape itself allowed both female and male workers to bond as a social group, to transcend former gender barriers, and to act instead as equal agents of progress in an imagined frontier.

The female workers had to negotiate their disruptions in this field—both with the men and among each other. The women had to overcome multilayered, complex gender expectations, and they did this successfully by using the ideas of the women's movement and empowering themselves through their engagement with the landscape.

Setting the Stage

That exclusionary cultural construction of the frontier, now set in Alaska, demanded that the women who worked the pipeline deal with the expectations and challenges of a geographic setting traditionally reserved for and defined by men. In the collective imagination of nineteenth-century America, the Western frontier was understood as a redemptive natural space that could provide spiritual salvation for those who would settle within it, as Henry Nash Smith argued in *Virgin Land.*[24]

Beginning with James Fenimore Cooper, writers of the American canon—which tends to reflect a nation's glorified version of itself—created protagonists following the model of the American Adam who succeeds without a traditional social background of the kind many European literature heroes shared. Instead, the American Adam was self-reliant, often living in harmony with nature.

Although the concept of the frontier and the figure of the American Adam certainly describe the mindset that guided interactions with the landscape—and the frontier narrative is a predominantly male-dominated genre— these concepts obscure and oversimplify the roles of women. Frontier women, if included at all, play mostly a negative role as reminders of the society and feminine domestication from which the American Adam was trying to escape.[25]

This gendered understanding of the frontier was fueled by myths about the heroic qualities of the frontiersman— qualities such as self-sufficiency, courage, bodily strength, individualism, and domination over nature.[26] Idolized figures like cowboys or gold miners and other frontiersmen are celebrated in American history and literature.[27]

The frontier myth shaped an understanding of history that would, among other things, marginalize women in its narrative. After the continental western frontier closed and the sources of the cultural heritage myths receded into history, geographical surrogates arose. These new spaces include outer space (the Final Frontier), the Middle East (thinking about the recent wars), and Alaska.[28]

During construction of the TAPS, newspapers often reminded readers of Alaska's role as a frontier—for example, the *Chicago Sun Times* compared the living conditions in the construction camps with the historic gold mining camps in the same area.[29] This constructed frontier setting influenced the workers' behavior, language, and self-perception. In the present book, for instance, Irene Bartee explains that the setup for surveying the pipeline route was "like the old-fashioned wagon trains out West."[30]

Ginger-Lei Collins, a young truck driver, mentioned in an interview her excitement that the job offered a "sense of adventure, of being part of America's last frontier."[31] Moreover, pipeline terms such as *bullcook* originated in the frontier setting. The term was used originally to describe the camp attendant and animal caretaker, and in the context of the TAPS, it describes the person looking after the sleeping quarters.

Thus, the frontier myth remained alive, and yet, despite the change in geography and the social advancements, the frontier construct left little room for diverse voices. In the collective memory, the metanarrative, and the general recollection of the workplace in Alaska's oil fields, women remained a marginalized group.

New Labor and the Cultures of the White Male Workplace

Not only was the perception of Alaska as a frontier and the pipeline construction as a male workplace challenged in the pipeline era, but also greater social changes advanced the standing of women in the workplace.

Following World War II, the white working class underwent a profound transformation: living standards improved significantly, high school graduation became the norm, and college enrollment tripled.[32] With women taking on jobs (that often paid significantly less), men's exclusive economic power declined, and, with this the role of working women in society began to accelerate.

In the 1960s and 1970s, the proportion of women in the workforce grew and women's concerns, therefore, began to gain momentum. During the pipeline construction, women had the opportunity to choose their own lifestyles and to diversify their roles. Along with an increased level of personal freedom came expectations for professional promotions. Donna Ford, a security officer, explains that after her divorce, she alone was responsible for herself—a situation that was initially difficult for some of her male coworkers to comprehend.[33]

The difficulties Ford encountered were anticipated by a key piece of legislation, the Equal Rights Amendment (ERA). The ERA was to guarantee equal education, training, and employment opportunities for women, as well as the elimination of discrimination based on sex. In fact, the ERA's first—and crucial—sentence reads: "Equality of rights under the law shall not be denied or abridged by the United States or by any State on account of sex."[34]

One might assume this amendment would face little opposition; however, it has yet to be ratified. The House of Representatives passed the ERA in 1972, and the Senate followed the same year. The legislation faced a variety of backlash, which centered mostly on the upholding of traditional family values, the perceived loss of status of women who worked outside the home, and especially on stories about the unhappiness of economically independent women. It has been documented how this conflict was fueled and constructed by the media's misinformation and disinformation.[35] To become part of the Constitution, however, the amendment needed to be ratified by thirty-eight states, and only thirty-one states have done so, since the ERA lacked public approval.

Alaska was among the first states to ratify the ERA, in 1972, with very little public debate.[36] Among other effects, this ratification ensured that successful and qualified female applicants for the TAPS construction crew had to be accommodated. Indeed, the federal Trans-Alaska Pipeline

Authorization Act of 1973 (TAPAA) includes an affirmative action clause, Section 403, which specifies:

> The Secretary of the Interior shall take such affirmative action as he deems necessary to assure that no person shall, on the grounds of race, creed, color, national origin, or sex, be excluded [from] any activity conducted under [the Trans-Alaska Pipeline Authorization Act].

By defining women as a minority, the TAPAA called for proactively favoring women on the job market. Whatever other challenges women might have faced, this gave them the opportunity to demonstrate their abilities in a professional environment.

Initially, the pipeline project witnessed a clash between what was prescribed in Section 403 and Alyeska's practice, as illustrated by the case of surveyor Glenda Straube, discussed in the local *All-Alaska Weekly*.[37] Before coming to the North Slope, Straube faced extraordinary obstacles that were only overcome by public pressure generated through strategic press coverage. With all the right union qualifications and the necessary training to work as part of a construction surveyor crew, Straube was hired to work at Atigun camp.

Following her successful bid, Straube was told to report for some orientation classes, which she completed. However, upon boarding the plane to reach her placement, she was informed there were no facilities for women at Atigun camp and that she could not be dispatched—although she would be fully paid until the matter was settled.

As Straube stated, "[Alyeska] denied me the right to go to a job and perform a job."[38] She saw her position repeatedly advertised in the Teamster union hall and came to realize she was the only qualified person for the placement.

With the support of her union and the press, Straube made a public statement: "Alyeska should have foreseen that times were changing and that women would be up there on the Slope."[39] Within a few hours, Straube was offered a position at Dietrich camp, where all facilities were ready, and she became the first Teamster woman to be dispatched to the Slope.

This example demonstrates that Alyeska had initially neglected to allow for the possibility the unions would hire women and that women actually would want to work on the pipeline construction. Straube was one of many women who were outspoken about the incipient troubles, and their forthrightness likely helped to resolve the issues.

At the beginning of the same month, Alyeska issued a "Policy on Employment of Women in Camps" that spoke of "increasing pressure" from women's organizations and individuals regarding possible employment opportunities.[40] The policy noted the camps had to be designed to accommodate women dispatched for work.

According to the company's vice president for construction, Peter Demay, it was initially assumed women would mostly work in clerical positions; therefore, only camps that required such workers had been designed to accommodate a female workforce.[41] Camps like Atigun hosted mostly welders, surveyors, dynamiters, and construction workers—all traditional male professions—and had no facilities for women.

One year later, in 1975, women were still challenging the stereotype that limited them to desk positions. One female dynamiter was quoted as having to fight "to pick up anything heavier than a piece of paper."[42]

In the present volume, Onice McClain notes she "was never very scared to speak up, so I wouldn't let them [male coworkers] get by with much . . ."[43]

This outspokenness and confidence increased participation in the workforce, and legislative support provided basic opportunities. Rising public awareness about discrimination provided further opportunities for the female workers to challenge the male workspace boundaries.

The Workers' Emerging Sense of Self and Representations

In the early stages of the TAPS construction, Alaska's image as a frontier stood in direct contrast to what was commonly understood as workplace and place for women in general. But, the advancing construction of the pipeline bore testimony to the fact that women's sense of self directly correlated with the erosion of the existing concept of masculinity in favor of the community. Whilst men tended to embrace work based on the characteristics of the American Adam, the project—because of its setting— favored the community approach that allowed women to enter the stage.

Katie Cotten elaborates in the present book that after initial difficulties, the workers in the project came to realize everyone was struggling with the harsh environment and the climatic conditions of Northern Alaska, and the common issues quickly began to override gender differences.[44]

According to Gloria Miller, who studied gender relations in the Canadian oil industry, masculinity is exercised in everyday interactions that informally exclude women and in competition that reinforces the division of labor. Miller interviewed mostly white-collar workers in supervisory positions, and she argues that gendered roles created a "web of assumptions" of the individual's abilities that made women invisible in the industry.[45]

She also alluded to social barriers at the personal level that hindered women and men from mingling in the camps, much like Donna Ford reports in her interview. However, the overall experiences of the women interviewed in this collection challenge Miller's observations of complications in the work environment arising from gender conflicts and "subtle, apparently caring, and protective *paternalism.*"[46]

Instead, Irene Bartee confidently and almost maternally recalls in her interview that she "never lost any men to the cold" and expresses her pride in the care she took for her coworkers.[47] Bartee also remembers that she "provided for [the other workers] and watched after them pretty seriously."[48]

In contrast to Miller's observations, the initial gender barrier based on typical frontier individualism was ultimately overcome during the pipeline construction. The workers felt responsible for each other and identified as a team rather than inscribing the top-down dynamic Miller observed.

As a result, the women's self-perceptions corresponded in some ways more to the American Adam than to traditional feminine roles and their associated places. Overcoming the expected gender role ultimately allowed the women to come to terms with their situated identity in Alaska. By adopting and relating to frontier conditions, the women could embrace their adventures in Alaska as opportunities to challenge existing social conventions.

Claiming the frontier myth and modifying it to suit a project that relied on teamwork helped the women overcome their initial insecurities concerning their abilities and empowered them to embrace their work in a challenging environment. Taking part in changing the perceived frontier enabled the women to identify as pioneers in the landscape as well as in the workplace, and at the same time, they were recognized by wider social structures as pioneering women.

There is a public celebration of these women as latter-day pioneers that still stands. The Pipeline Monument in Valdez, which was unveiled in September 1980, shows that the pipeline service company encourages the acceptance of women in the male sphere of work and in the frontier. The thirteen-foot-tall bronze monument that stands inside the gate to the Alyeska Pipeline Terminal represents the workforce that built the TAPS.[49]

Malcolm Alexander, who won the competition to design the monument, wanted to honor the many faces of the pipeline's workforce. The monument commemorates "Twentieth Century Pioneers" and the "larger-than-life qualities demanded of the pipeline planners and builders—bravery, strength, tenacity, confidence, and imagination."[50] These personified qualities celebrate the traditional myth of the frontier, and, at the same time, the figures themselves schematize the workers who participated in the pipeline construction—identified on the plaque as a surveyor, a welder, an indigenous workman, and a female Teamster.

The monument takes an innovative approach to the understanding of Alaska as a frontier by paying tribute to indigenous workers, usually framed more as victims than as pioneers. Indigenous peoples represented 14 to 19 percent of the workforce and significantly contributed to Alaska's oil industry.[51]

Also innovative is the tribute to women, who made up between 5 and 10 percent of the overall pipeline construction workforce, and about half of the women working on the project held blue-collar jobs.[52]

Therefore, Alyeska's monument reflects the diversity of the pipeline construction workers—neither exclusively white nor exclusively male—and fosters the image of its multiracial and mixed-gender workforce as pioneers.

An Alyeska-commissioned photo collection of the pipeline workforce by Neal Menschel and Ken Roberts further emphasizes women working in a traditionally male workplace. The images are mostly close-up portraits of predominantly female employees posing on their workstations; the photographs visually disintegrate gender barriers by highlighting that women were working in traditional masculine jobs.

While not renouncing the hard hat or standard uniform, the women also sustain femininity by wearing jewelry, makeup, and nail polish. Rather than embracing the masculine side of their job identity, these women—as framed by Alyeska—champion certain aspects of their gender and simultaneously push the boundaries of the typical gender roles of their time.

Enabled by the constructed landscape qualities of Alaska as a place for the American Adam, female workers helped "trailblaze" a way of life that transcended gender to create a new model for the American working class. Interestingly, this role was imposed by Alyeska and modified the workers' image to suit the frontier myth rather than confronting and challenging the myth itself.

Alyeska's imagery constructed the female workers as courageous, independent women whose bodily strength enabled domination of nature. The imagery implies, on the one hand, a change in the concept of the frontier and the character of the person inhabiting it, and, on the other hand, an assimilation of the values of the women's movement into Alyeska's agenda.

As the female figure on the monument in Valdez and the women in the photographs demonstrate, the (mostly white) female worker was eventually embraced at Alyeska. In a 1976 interview, Jim Wagner, the acting camp manager in Coldfoot, stated that the camps had "passed the stage of resistance to women up here."[53]

Other interviews from the same period also convey a progressive attitude. Ginger-Lei Collins, a nineteen-year-old truck driver, told the *San Francisco Chronicle*: "Show me what to do and I'll do it," and she confidently asserted that she was "not going to take any s— from anyone. I do my job. I don't slack off."[54]

Roxie (Hollingsworth) Majeske summarizes her experience on the North Slope in the present book by saying, "You had to be strong. . . . I did what everybody else did. I didn't ever let it stop me that I was a woman."[55] Both female and male workers had to accept vulnerability and strength as factors that were not gender-specific to overcome challenges presented by the harsh environment.

The official endorsement of female workers in the Alaska oil industry fed back into a zeitgeist already occupied with women's rights. All the public discussions of the pipeline women point to the "same work, same pay" policy and to the conventions of gender equality that were enforced on the pipeline.

A woman interviewed by KMBC-TV explained that it was easier to sleep and relax in a mixed barrack, which she preferred to an all-female facility, since the arrangement gave her the opportunity to get to know all the other workers.[56] For workers in an occupation that combines high risks with small-team organization, such as the oil industry, the group's safety depended on establishing mutual trust and commitment to the team.

The setting of Alaska and nature of the pipeline project itself aided the dismantlement of the frontier as exclusively male space because self-reliance and individualism were undesirable within the project. The new pioneers had to be gender- and race-inclusive and work in teams to successfully complete the pipeline.

As some of the women observed, the hazardous environment challenged both genders equally. This profound equality, rooted in human vulnerability against the elements, informed the evolving sense of both the men and women working on the pipeline. The oil pioneers in Alaska recognized themselves as living on a new northern frontier and were further constructed through frontier characteristics by Alyeska and the media for the wider public. Moreover, this image suited the general zeitgeist concerned with the advancing recognition of women in the workplace and society.

Questions of Equal Treatment

In 1974, construction worker Nancy Ribbik described herself as "no women's libber" in an interview with the *Fairbanks Daily News-Miner*, but she argued that "everybody should have a chance to do what they're capable of doing."[57]

The women interviewed in this book emphasize that their aim was to be able to choose their own lifestyle; they were living out a powerful cultural narrative enabled by the nationwide social changes and the collective imagination of what Alaska was. The visual and verbal documentation of the women workers infiltrated the concept of the new pioneer and subverted the company's use of the women's images by drawing attention to their achievement— framed as pioneering. That attention to achievement was an important step forward.

Earlier, in the 1960s, American women organized themselves in national movements that drew attention to their unequal role in society. On the oil fields, equal rights issues included concerns that might not immediately come to mind, such as washroom facilities and sleeping arrangements, as well as familiar issues, such as promotions and respectful treatment.[58]

In this context, it is fascinating to read about Irene Bartee, who refers to herself in the present book not merely as an equal part of a team, but as a leading figure in the male-dominated work community.[59] Similarly, Iñupiat Alaska Native Debora Strutz, who worked as a driver, speaks of "build[ing] a family of pipeline workers."[60] Her story relates her struggles as one of a small number of women among the workers, which she overcame, and she recalls that "[e]verybody felt like they were taken care of and they would take care of the other guys" like a family.[61]

One year into the construction, an Alyeska report based on internal interviews with female and male workers about women in construction notes that the male workers' initial skepticism was met and overcome by women with exceptional work ethics. The senior project manager stated that, as a result, "views have changed from anti-women in camps to very definitely *pro*."[62]

The role of women on the pipeline would be exaggerated if men were overlooked. Then, as now, the resource-extracting labor market was mostly male in its composition and masculine in its assumptions and values.[63] As the interviews in this collection demonstrate, the women's work perceptions were heavily influenced by interactions with their coworkers. Moreover, an approach focusing on women alone tends to view the genders as opposing groups and overlook the fact that as workers, they are united stakeholders.

Like his female counterpart, the male worker was also stereotyped, and his behavior constructed accordingly. "[T]he heavily masculinized oil industry is seen as the ultimate site for machismo," note Anahita and Mix.[64] The presence of women may have even reinforced the masculinity of the industry's male workers. In her interview, Rosemary Carroll concludes with admiration for her coworkers—male and female—and challenges this notion of separation by stating that she felt a sense of unity among the workers.[65] Working in Alaska's harsh environment, the workers' safety depended on establishing mutual trust that moved beyond gender.

The social changes of the 1970s and the understanding of Alaska as a frontier positively influenced attitudes, interactions, and policies concerning women contributing to the pipeline construction. The workers overcame stereotyped assumptions of gender, and this success provides valuable insights into ways in which occupations that were usually gender-segregated were being transformed in the 1970s, as well as what equal employment can mean in the future.

The collected interviews in this volume help unpack the social construction of womanhood in the oil industry, not as mere symbol and stereotype in a certain rough-hewn work culture, but as part of a new, multigendered workplace. The interviews collected by Williams provide important documentation of the necessary adjustments—such as changes to housing arrangements—that are still relevant to contemporary mining operations.

The narratives about the pipeline, framed in a frontier setting, encourage Americans to live deliberately by reconnecting with the nation's history, gathering courage, taking risks, and facing societal changes rather than fearing them. Finally, this book should not be read as the underside of the pipeline history—instead, it reminds us to pay attention to those to whom a voice is given.

Julia Feuer-Cotter, is a geographer and environmental historian studying gendered environmental interactions in the Arctic. She has spent considerable time in Alaska researching current and former female pipeline workers' understanding of the environment through archival work, interviews, and workshops.

GLOSSARY

Alaska Native/Natives—Indigenous peoples of Alaska from the Iñupiat, Yup'ik, Aleut, Eyak, Tlingit, Haida, Tsimshian, and Northern Athabaskan cultures.

ARCO—Atlantic Richfield Company.

ATCO units—Construction trailers that vary in size, but are generally twelve feet by forty feet.

Aztec—Four- to six-seat, twin-engine light aircraft.

baleen—Filter inside whale mouths.

bullcook—A housekeeping job—making beds, vacuuming, changing sheets, dusting.

bunny boots—Extreme cold, vapor-barrier boots used by the US armed forces. The boots retain heat through layers of wool and felt insulation between two layers of rubber.

cat trains—A Caterpiller pulling ATCO trailers over the snowy tundra.

call-out—During the day, Alaska unions provided workers with times when they would announce the names of people who got jobs. People would put their names on call lists. If you had just come off a job, your name would go to the bottom of the appropriate list. People would work themselves from the C and D lists to the B and A lists by working. People from the A list were hired first, then B, C, and, in some unions, D. People who had never worked would be on the C or D list. If a person was not in the hall at the time his name was called, he might lose out on the job. In the early days of the pipeline, there were so many jobs that the calls would extend to the C and D list.

conductor—Surface pipe.

CPF (central processing facility)—Facility where the pipelines conjoin for processing oil.

connex—Portable, metal shipping container.

D8—Large track-type bulldozer made by Caterpillar.

dispatch—When a person is the next name on a union list for an open position and is asked to contact the employer to begin work for a union contractor.

downhole—Inside the well pipe.

drill site—An accumulation of wells on a compacted gravel pad, approximately ten to twenty acres.

E-line—Electrical cable used to lower and retrieve wellbore tools.

ear pull—A game where two people face each other and a leather cord is strung between two of the players' ears. Each player pulls until either the cord comes free or a player quits due to pain. This game is often not performed any longer due to safety concerns.

ESD (emergency shutdown)—When a process is stopped, usually by a valve or multiple valves, due to an emergency.

firing line—Where the welding is being accomplished on the pipe on pipeline projects.

gathering center—Facility that processes raw crude oil and forwards the processed oil to the Trans-Alaska Pipeline. These facilities have multiple names depending upon location, such as *central processing facility* and *flow station*.

grease head—Piece of equipment that sits on the lubricator, designed to contain well pressure while running the braided cable into or out of the well.

haul road—A shortened name used for the 414-mile James W. Dalton Highway, also referred to as the Dalton Highway and the North Slope Haul Road. The mostly gravel road begins north of Fairbanks at the Elliot Highway and extends to Deadhorse.

HR—Human Resources.

ice road—A winter road created with layers of ice, which is on top of a frozen water surface or land, such as Alaska tundra. The road provides a flat, smooth driving surface and protects the land underneath from destruction.

Iñupiat—The Iñupiat live in Northern Alaska from Norton Sound on the Bering Sea to Canada on the east. Iñupiat people have lived in the area for thousands of years. People were moved from sod huts to aboveground wooden houses in the twentieth century.

KOC (Kuparuk Operations Camp)—Living quarters for operations personnel at Kuparuk.

movie reels—Round reels containing movie film.

knuckle hop—Game where a contestant takes the push-up position and hops forward on toes and knuckles. The person that goes the farthest wins.

MCC—Main Construction Camp—also Prime Camp—Living quarters for contractors at Prudhoe Bay.

mukluks—High, soft boots traditionally made of seal skin.

musk ox—Arctic mammal known for its thick coat.

pad—Parking area constructed of compacted gravel placed on top of the Arctic tundra.

PBOC (Prudhoe Bay Operations Camp)—Living quarters at Prudhoe Bay for operations personnel.

PE—Physical Education.

Pet 4—Created in 1923 and originally named Naval Petroleum Reserve Number 4, this reserve is now entitled National Petroleum Reserve in Alaska (NPRA). It is where oil is known to exist. The US government started leasing tracks to oil companies in the late 1990s.

pingo—Mound of earth-covered ice.

PPE—Personal protection equipment, such as hard hat, safety glasses, and ear plugs.

Prime Camp—Also known as Slime Camp. Living quarters for construction workers.

Prudhoe Bay Follies—An entertainment show at Prudhoe Bay.

PSV—Pressure safety valve.

ptarmigan—A medium-sized gamebird in the grouse family.

R&R—Rest and recuperation period in which employees work seven days a week on the North Slope and then are sent home for relaxation.

recip—Short for *reciprocating*. A reciprocating compressor is a piston compressor delivering gases at high pressure.

Refrigiwear—Brand name of insulated, cold-weather work gear.

stab-in and bolting—The act of guiding components that couple, such as placing the male threads of a piece of the drillstring into the mating female threads and then tightening.

sandjetting—Removing sand and particles from a production separator.

sealift—When the Arctic Ocean is open enough to allow barges to come through the ice and deliver materials and prefabricated buildings built at construction sites in the Lower 48.

slickline—Wire or cable used to put tools into a well or recover equipment in the well, such as gauges and plugs.

Slime Camp—One of the original construction camps at Prudhoe Bay.

snow snake—Drifting snow swirling around at the ground level.

South 48—Also called Lower 48, meaning the states in the continental United States.

spirit bag—Necklace that can have herbs sewn inside and worn for spiritual protection.

Surfcoat—Protective coating used on pipe.

TAPS—Trans-Alaska Pipeline System.

trees—Surface pipe that holds equipment, such as valves and instruments, from at least fifteen feet to as much as thirty feet high.

waterflood—Pushing water underground to flush oil to nearby producing wells.

whiteout—A snow condition in which visibility and contrast are severely reduced. On the North Slope, the dry snow blows horizontally and the horizon disappears. There are no or few reference points visible below a certain height. Generally, a 966 or 988 loader or taller vehicle can see above whiteout conditions. There are three phases of whiteout: Phase 1 indicates caution driving with individual vehicles; Phase 2 indicates travel in a convoy of vehicles that can communicate among each other; and Phase 3 indicates road travel is prohibited, except for emergency vehicles.

ENDNOTES

1 Alaska Oil and Gas Conservation Commission, "Oil and Gas Pool Statistics," 2011, http://doa.alaska.gov/ogc/annual/current/18_oil_pools/katalla%20undefined%20-%20 oil/1_oil_1.htm?_ga=2.211653781.1236785597.1516396973-2143283254.1516396973.

2 P. Coates, *The Trans-Alaska Pipeline Controversy* (London: Associated University Press, 1991).

3 W. R. Borneman, *Alaska: Saga of a Bold Land* (New York: Perennial, 2003).

4 Ibid.

5 Ibid.

6 Ibid.

7 Alyeska Pipeline Service Company, "Employment," Alyeska Pipeline Service Company, accessed March 21, 2015, http://www.alyeska-pipeline.com/TAPS/PipelineFacts.

8 Alyeska Pipeline Service Company, *Trans Alaska Pipeline System: The Facts* (Anchorage, AK: Alyeska Pipeline Service Company, 2016).

9 Alyeska Pipeline Service Company, "Employment."

10 Ibid.

11 *Milwaukee Business Journal*, "Steinem: More Work on Women's Issues," March 2, 2012, https://www.bizjournals.com/milwaukee/print-edition/2012/03/02/steinem-more-work-on-womens-issues.html.

12 V. Wallis, *Raising Ourselves* (Kenmore, WA: Epicenter Press, 2002), 13.

13 N. Nohria, interview by Charlie Rose, *Charlie Rose*, PBS, January 22, 2015.

14   E. Parlapiano, "Catalyst 2013 Census of Fortune 500: Still No Progress after Years of No Progress," Catalyst: Changing Workplaces, Changing Lives, Catalyst, Inc., accessed December 10, 2013, http://www.catalyst.org/media/catalyst-2013-census-fortune-500-still-no-progress-after-years-no-progress.

15   J. A. Dlouhy, "Energy Companies Have Work to Do in Recruiting Women," review of NES Global Talent Survey, *Houston Chronicle*, accessed March 12, 2014, Women-in-engineering-report-single_final-1.pdf.

16   D. Cole, *Amazing Pipeline Stories: How Building the Trans-Alaska Pipeline Transformed Life in America's Last Frontier* (Fairbanks, AK: Epicenter Press, 1997), 49.

17   M. P. Hogan and T. Pursell, "The 'Real Alaskan': Nostalgia and Rural Masculinity in the Last Frontier," *Men and Masculinities* 11, no. 1 (2008): 63–85.

18   J. Kleinfeld, *Frontier Romance: Environment, Culture, and Alaska Identity* (Fairbanks: University of Alaska Press, 2012).

19   S. Kollin, *Nature's State: Imagining Alaska as the Last Frontier* (Chapel Hill: University of North Carolina Press, 2001).

20   Cf. Kollin, *Nature's State*; Hogan and Pursell, "The 'Real Alaskan.'"

21   R. W. B. Lewis, *The American Adam: Innocence, Tragedy, and Tradition in the Nineteenth Century* (Chicago: University of Chicago Press, 1955).

22   Alyeska Pipeline Service Company, *Trans Alaska Pipeline System: The Facts* (Anchorage, AK: Alyeska Pipeline Service Company, 2016), www.alyeska-pipe.com/assets/uploads/pagestructure/TAPS_PipelineFacts/editor_uploads/2016FactBook.pdf.

23   Ibid.

24   H. Nash Smith, *Virgin Land: The American West as Symbol and Myth* (Cambridge, MA: Harvard University Press, 1970).

25   M. S. Kimmel, *Manhood in America: A Cultural History* (New York: Free Press, 1996).

26   S. Anahita and T. L. Mix, "Retrofitting Frontier Masculinities for Alaska's War against Wolves," *Gender and Society* 20, no. 3 (2006), 332–53.

27   R. Connell, *Masculinities* (Cambridge, UK: Polity, 2005).

28   Kimmel, *Manhood in America*.

29   K. Brown, "Women Invade Male Bastion in Arctic," *Sun Times Chicago*, 1976.

30 I. Bartee, interview by Carla Williams, Carla Williams Private Collection, Anchorage, 2016 [1999].

31 R. Stein, "She Works on the Pipeline," *San Francisco Chronicle*, 1976.

32 E. Boris and N. Lichtenstein, *Major Problems in the History of American Workers* (Boston: Wadsworth, 2003), 432.

33 D. Ford, interview by Carla Williams, Carla Williams Private Collection, Anchorage, 2016 [1999].

34 R. Francis, ERA Task Force for the National Council of Women's Organizations, "The Equal Rights Amendment," 2013, www.equalrightsamendment.org/history.htm.

35 S. Faludi, *Backlash: The Undeclared War against American Women* (New York: Crown Publishing, 1991).

36 J. K. Boles, *The Politics of the Equal Rights Amendment* (New York: Longman, 1979).

37 "Mother of Two Dispatched to Slope as a Surveyor," *All-Alaska Weekly*, May 24, 1974.

38 Ibid.

39 Ibid.

40 G. H. Lundell, "Alyeska Policy on Employment of Women in Camps," Carla Williams Private Collection, Anchorage, 1974.

41 P. Demay, "Subject: Alyeska Policy on Women: Employment in Camps," Carla Williams Private Collection, Anchorage, 1974.

42 D. Simmons, "Women Fight for the Right to Lift More Than a Piece of Paper," *Daily News-Miner*, Fairbanks, 1975.

43 O. McClain, interview by Carla Williams, Carla Williams Private Collection, Anchorage, 2016 [1999].

44 Kate Cotten, interview by Carla Williams, Carla Williams Private Collection, Anchorage, 2016 [1998].

45 G. E. Miller, "Frontier Masculinity in the Oil Industry: The Experience of Women Engineers," *Gender, Work, and Organization* 11 (2004), 47–73, 70.

46 Ibid, p. 49.

47 Bartee, interview by Carla Williams.

48 Ibid.

49 I want to thank Coates's study of the TAPS controversy for making me aware of the monument.

50 P. A. Coates, *The Trans-Alaska Pipeline Controversy: Technology, Conversation, and the Frontier* (Bethlehem, PA: Lehigh University Press, 1991), 318.

51 Alyeska Pipeline Service Company, "Employment," Alyeska Pipeline Service Company, accessed March 21, 2015, http:// www.alyeska-pipeline.com/TAPS/PipelineFacts.

52 Cole, *Amazing Pipeline Stories.*

53 Brown, "Women Invade Male Bastion in Arctic."

54 Stein, "She Works on the Pipeline."

55 R. Hollingsworth, interview by Carla Williams, Carla Williams Private Collection, Anchorage, 2016 [1999].

56 KMBC-TV, newsservice manuscript, "Alaska Pipeline," Carla Williams Private Collection, Anchorage, 1975.

57 "First Woman Worker Heads for the North Slope," *Fairbanks Daily News-Miner,* 1974.

58 *Women in Construction: Use of Women in the Construction Work Force,* staff report prepared for F. Moolin, Helen Atkinson papers, Archives, Alaska and Polar Regions Collections, Rasmuson Library, University of Alaska Fairbanks, Box 1, unpublished, undated.

59 Bartee, interview by Carla Williams.

60 D. Strutz, interview by Carla Williams, Carla Williams Private Collection, Anchorage, 2016 [2010].

61 Ibid.

62 *Women in Construction: Use of Women in the Construction Work Force,* staff report prepared for F. Moolin, Helen Atkinson papers, Archives, Alaska and Polar Regions Collections, Rasmuson Library, University of Alaska Fairbanks, Box 1, unpublished, undated.

63 Miller, "Frontier Masculinity in the Oil Industry."

64 Anahita and Mix, "Retrofitting Frontier Masculinities for Alaska's War against Wolves," 334.

65 R. Carroll, interview with Carla Williams, Carla Williams Private Collection, Anchorage, 2016 [1999].

INDEX

ABOUT THE AUTHOR

Like so many other baby boomers of her era, Carla Williams arrived in Anchorage the summer of 1974. She remembers rarely seeing anyone over forty in those years.

Young people arrived in droves week after week, causing a flourishing environment. Rents skyrocketed, so she started her adventure outside of Anchorage in Chugiak in a one-room cabin with an outhouse and an oil lamp. She shared an old truck with her boyfriend, so sometimes she had to hitchhike to the big city.

With her boyfriend working as a summer surveyor in Alaska, she planned to come for the summer and return to Santa Barbara, California, in the fall. However, good-paying jobs and the excitement of those early pipeline days kept her in Alaska.

Carla grew up in Crosby, Minnesota, the daughter of a jeweler and legal secretary. She started working in the family jewelry store at ten years old, cleaning, waiting on customers, and decorating the store windows with her Barbie doll collection. After graduating from high school, she moved to Santa Barbara, where she performed bookkeeping and attended Santa Barbara City College. Her dream was to live the Southern California lifestyle, but Alaska beckoned and she answered the call.

While in Alaska, she married twice and had a son, Shane. She lived in both Anchorage and Fairbanks and graduated from the University of Alaska Fairbanks with a bachelor of arts degree in English and a minor in elementary education. She taught in Fairbanks as a substitute teacher, but left the profession to return to the oil and gas industry when her second husband, Don, was transferred to Anchorage with his job.

In 1990, she underwent surgery and chemotherapy for Stage Two breast cancer and worked tirelessly for more than ten years as a breast cancer advocate in Anchorage, Juneau, and Washington, D.C., with the National Breast Cancer Coalition. She was recognized by Alaska governor Frank Murkowski for her advocacy work in helping to pass the breast cancer treatment legislation in Alaska, which offers breast cancer treatment to underserved women.

She worked in various jobs in Alaska, including teaching, office management, writing, accounting, engineering, sales, and quality management. She spent most of her career working in the Alaska oil and gas industry, in Anchorage and the North Slope.

Carla and Don met on a PRICE/CIRI construction project on the North Slope in the mid-1980s, where Don was the project engineer, and they have been together ever since. They recently moved to Sedona, Arizona, where they enjoy partial retirement and hiking the red rocks. Carla works as a hiking guide for Enchantment Resort in Sedona.